# MATHFOCUS 5

## Workbook

**Senior Author and Senior Consultant**
Marian Small

**Authors**
Carol Brydon
Elizabeth Grill-Donovan
Jack Hope
Wendy Klassen
Marian Small
Susan Stuart
Rosita Tseng Tam

**Workbook Author**
Christy Hayhoe

**Assessment Consultants**
Sandra Carl Townsend
Gerry Varty

NELSON EDUCATION

# NELSON EDUCATION

## Nelson Math Focus 5 Workbook

**Senior Author and Senior Consultant**
Marian Small

**Student Book Authors**
Carol Brydon, Elizabeth Grill-Donovan, Jack Hope, Wendy Klassen, Marian Small, Susan Stuart, Rosita Tseng Tam

**Workbook Author**
Christy Hayhoe

**Assessment Consultants**
Sandra Carl Townsend
Gerry Varty

**Director of Publishing**
Kevin Martindale

**General Manager, Mathematics, Science & Technology**
Lenore Brooks

**Publisher, Mathematics**
Colin Garnham

**Associate Publisher, Mathematics**
Sandra McTavish

**Managing Editor, Development**
David Spiegel

**Product Manager**
Linda Krepinsky

**Program Manager**
Mary Reeve

**Developmental Editors**
Shirley Barrett
Christy Hayhoe

**Executive Director, Content and Media Production**
Renate McCloy

**Director, Content and Media Production**
Sujata Singh

**Content Production Manager, Mathematics**
Debbie Davies-Wright

**Content Production Editor**
Jane High

**Copy Editor**
Sandra Manley

**Proofreader**
Linda Szostak

**Production Manager**
Helen Jager Locsin

**Production Coordinator**
Kathrine Pummell

**Design Director**
Ken Phipps

**Interior Design**
Greg Devitt
Eugene Lo
Peter Papayanakis

**Cover Design**
Eugene Lo

**Cover Image**
Illin Sergey/Shutterstock

**Illustrators**
Jennifer Loates
Dave Whamond

**Compositor**
Janet Zanette

**COPYRIGHT © 2009** by Nelson Education Ltd.

ISBN-13: 978-0-17-632456-8
ISBN-10: 0-17-632456-9

Printed in Canada.
7   15

For more information contact Nelson Education Ltd., 1120 Birchmount Road, Toronto, Ontario, M1K 5G4. Or you can visit our Internet site at http://www.nelson.com

**ALL RIGHTS RESERVED.** No part of this work covered by the copyright herein, except for any reproducible pages included in this work, may be reproduced, transcribed, or used in any form or by any means— graphic, electronic, or mechanical, including photocopying, recording, taping, Web distribution, or information storage and retrieval systems— without the written permission of the publisher.

For permission to use material from this text or product, submit all requests online at www.cengage.com/permissions

Further questions about permissions can be emailed to permissionrequest@cengage.com

Every effort has been made to trace ownership of all copyrighted material and to secure permission from copyright holders. In the event of any question arising as to the use of any material, we will be pleased to make the necessary corrections in future printings.

Reproduction of BLMs is permitted for classroom/instruction purposes only and only to the purchaser of this product.

# Contents

**Message to Parent/Guardian**     iv

| CHAPTER 1 | Patterns in Mathematics | 1 |
| CHAPTER 2 | Numeration | 10 |
| CHAPTER 3 | Adding and Subtracting Decimals | 21 |
| CHAPTER 4 | Data Relationships | 30 |
| CHAPTER 5 | Motion Geometry | 37 |
| CHAPTER 6 | Multiplication | 43 |
| CHAPTER 7 | Fractions | 55 |
| CHAPTER 8 | Measurement | 64 |
| CHAPTER 9 | Division | 75 |
| CHAPTER 10 | Probability | 86 |
| CHAPTER 11 | 2-D and 3-D Geometry | 93 |

# Message to Parent/Guardian

This workbook has one page of practice questions for each lesson in the Student Book for *Nelson Math Focus 5*. The questions in the workbook are similar to the ones in the Student Book, so they should look familiar to your child. The lesson Goal and the At-Home Help on each page will help you to provide support if your child needs it.

At the end of each chapter is a page of multiple-choice questions called "Test Yourself." This is an opportunity for you and your child to see how well she or he understands.

You can help your child explore and understand math ideas by making available some commonly found materials, such as

- toothpicks (for patterns)
- pennies, dimes, quarters, and loonies (for number operations)
- counters such as buttons or coins (for number operations)
- tracing paper and scissors (for geometry and fractions)
- cubes, a transparent mirror, and pencil crayons (for geometry)
- grid paper (for multiplication)
- ruler and metre stick (for measurement)
- water and a variety of measuring cups and spoons (for measurement)
- several empty containers (for measurement)
- paper clip and sharp pencil (for probability)

Visit the Nelson website at **www.nelson.com/mathfocus** to find out more about the mathematics your child is learning.

It's amazing what you can learn when you look at math through your child's eyes! Here are some things you might watch for.

**Checklist**
- ☑ Can your child clearly explain her or his thinking?
- ☑ Does your child check to see whether an answer makes sense?
- ☑ Does your child persevere until the work is complete?
- ☑ Does your child connect new concepts to what has already been learned?
- ☑ Is your child proud of what's been accomplished so far?

# Chapter 1 Lesson 1: Modelling Patterns

**GOAL**

Use models to represent, extend, and make predictions about number patterns.

You will need toothpicks and pennies.

1. Rebecca made a pattern using toothpicks and pennies. Then she started a number table.

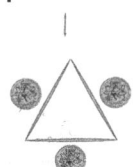  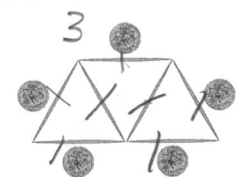

1  2  3

**At-Home Help**

A **pattern rule** is a description of how a pattern starts and how it continues.

For the pattern 2, 6, 10, 14, …, the pattern rule is "Start at 2 and add 4 each time."

a) Fill in the shaded cells of Rebecca's number table.

| Number of triangles | 1 | 2 | 3 | 4 | 5 | 6 | 7 |
|---|---|---|---|---|---|---|---|
| Number of toothpicks | 3 | 5 | 7 | 9 | 11 | 13 | 15 |
| Number of pennies | 3 | 4 | 5 | 6 | 7 | 8 | 9 |

b) Use toothpicks and pennies to extend Rebecca's pattern up to four triangles. Sketch your model.

c) What is the pattern rule for the number of toothpicks?

   _skip cont by 3_

   What is the pattern rule for the number of pennies?

   _skip cont by 2_

d) Predict the number of pennies needed for five triangles.

   __7__ pennies

   Make a model to check. Sketch your model.

e) Extend the pattern for up to seven triangles. Then complete the number table above.

# Chapter 1 Lesson 2: Extending Increasing Patterns

**GOAL**

Describe and extend increasing number patterns.

1. What is a pattern rule for each pattern?

   a) 1, 3, 5, 7, ...
   Pattern rule: _add 2 each time_

   b) 5, 10, 15, ...
   Pattern rule: _add 5 each time_

   c) 12, 22, 32, ...
   Pattern rule: _add 10 each time_

2. Fill in the next three numbers in each pattern.

   a) 2, 3, 4, _5_, _8_, _7_

   b) 20, 25, 30, _35_, _40_, _45_

   c) 3, 6, 9, _12_, _15_, _18_

**At-Home Help**

In an increasing number pattern, each number is greater than the number before.
- 10, 11, 12, ... is an increasing number pattern. The pattern rule is "Start at 10 and add 1 each time."
- 50, 100, 150, 200, ... is an increasing number pattern. The pattern rule is "Start at 50 and add 50 each time."

3. Kate made a table to show the ingredients for chocolate macaroons.

   a) Extend Kate's pattern for up to five batches. Fill in the table.

| Number of batches | Butter (mL) | Chocolate squares | Coconut (mL) |
|---|---|---|---|
| 1 | 100 | 5 | 250 |
| 2 | 200 | 10 | 500 |
| 3 | 300 | 15 | 750 |
| 4 | 400 | 20 | 1000 |
| 5 | 500 | 25 | 1250 |

   b) Write each pattern rule.

   Pattern rule for butter: _____

   Pattern rule for chocolate squares: _____

   Pattern rule for coconut: _____

# Chapter 1 Lesson 3: Extending Decreasing Patterns

**GOAL**

Describe and extend decreasing number patterns.

**At-Home Help**

In a decreasing number pattern, each number is less than the number before.
- 50, 40, 30, ... is a decreasing number pattern. The pattern rule is "Start at 50 and subtract 10 each time."
- 20, 18, 16, 14, ... is a decreasing number pattern. The pattern rule is "Start at 20 and subtract 2 each time."

1. What is a pattern rule for each pattern?

    a) 10, 8, 6, ...
    Pattern rule: _dec 2 each time_

    b) 15, 14, 13, ...
    Pattern rule: _dec 1 each time_

    c) 90, 85, 80, ...
    Pattern rule: _dec 5 each time_

2. Fill in the next three numbers in each pattern.

    a) 77, 76, 75, _74_, _73_, _72_

    b) 1000, 900, 800, _700_, _600_, _500_

    c) 24, 20, 16, _12_, _8_, _4_

3. Owen is packing his collection of 150 comic books into boxes. 10 comics fit in each box. Owen created a pattern to show the number of boxes he needs. His pattern is 150, 140, 130, ....

    a) Why do the numbers in Owen's pattern decrease by 10 each time?
    _only 10 fit in 1 box each time_

    b) What is Owen's pattern rule? _dec by 10 each time_

    c) How many boxes does Owen need? _15_ boxes

4. Jay bought 47 jelly beans. Starting the next day, he ate 5 jelly beans every day. How many days did it take for Jay to eat all the jelly beans?
    _9 days remander 2_

# Chapter 1 Lesson 4: Describing Number Patterns in Games

**GOAL**

Create a number pattern game and describe the patterns.

1. Shanti, Kate, and Mateo are playing a number pattern game on a 100 chart. Shanti moves 2 spaces each turn. Kate moves 5 spaces each turn. Mateo moves 3 spaces each turn. The person who passes 100 first wins the game.

   | 1 | 2 | 3 | 4 | 5 | 6 | 7 | 8 | 9 | 10 |
   |---|---|---|---|---|---|---|---|---|---|
   | 11 | 12 | 13 | 14 | 15 | 16 | 17 | 18 | 19 | 20 |
   | 21 | 22 | 23 | 24 | 25 | 26 | 27 | 28 | 29 | 30 |
   | 31 | 32 | 33 | 34 | 35 | 36 | 37 | 38 | 39 | 40 |
   | 41 | 42 | 43 | 44 | 45 | 46 | 47 | 48 | 49 | 50 |
   | 51 | 52 | 53 | 54 | 55 | 56 | 57 | 58 | 59 | 60 |
   | 61 | 62 | 63 | 64 | 65 | 66 | 67 | 68 | 69 | 70 |
   | 71 | 72 | 73 | 74 | 75 | 76 | 77 | 78 | 79 | 80 |
   | 81 | 82 | 83 | 84 | 85 | 86 | 87 | 88 | 89 | 90 |
   | 91 | 92 | 93 | 94 | 95 | 96 | 97 | 98 | 99 | 100 |

   a) Shanti starts at 10. What number is she on after 3 turns? __16__

   b) Kate starts at 2. What number is she on after 3 turns? __17__

   c) Mateo starts at 4. What number is he on after 3 turns? __13__

   d) Write a pattern rule for each player.
   Shanti's pattern rule: __Start at 10 move 2 each time__
   Kate's pattern rule: __Start at 2 move 5 each time__
   Mateo's pattern rule: __Start at 4 move 3 each time__

   e) Predict who will win the game. Explain your thinking.
   _____

   f) Model the game. Who wins? _____

4  Nelson Math Focus 5 Workbook                                   Copyright © 2009 by Nelson Education Ltd.

# Solving Problems Using Patterns

**GOAL**

Identify patterns to solve problems.

1. Owen is counting his penny collection. He arranged the pennies in a triangle.

   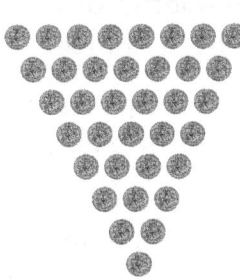

   a) What is the sum of the top and bottom rows? _____ pennies

   b) How can you use a pattern to count the pennies?
   _Start at 8 Sub by 1_
   _____

   c) How many pennies does Owen have?
   _36_

**At-Home Help**

You can use patterns to figure out the sum of numbers. How many marbles are there?

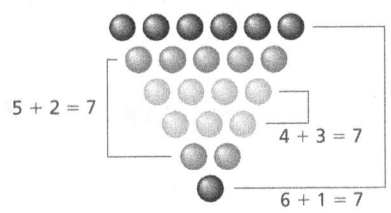

5 + 2 = 7
4 + 3 = 7
6 + 1 = 7

The sum of the top and bottom rows is 7.
The sum of the second top and bottom rows is 7.
The sum of the two middle rows is 7.
7 + 7 + 7 = 21
There are 21 marbles.

2. What is the sum of the numbers in the pattern 2, 4, 6, 8, 10, 12, 14, 16? Sydney calculates 2 + 16 = 18. Use a pattern to finish Sydney's work.

   _____
   _____

3. Calculate the sum of the numbers in each pattern.

   a) 5, 10, 15, 20, 25, 30
   
   Sum: _____
   
   b) 10, 9, 8, 7, 6, 5, 4, 3, 2, 1
   
   Sum: _____

# Chapter 1 Lesson 6
# Describing Relationships Using Expressions

**GOAL**

Use variables in expressions.

1. Brandon is going to visit his grandparents in 7 days from today. He wrote an expression for the date he is leaving: $t + 7$.

   a) What does the $t$ represent?

   _to_

   b) Why is the number 7 in the expression?

   _he is going to visit his grandparents in 7 day's_

   **At-Home Help**

   A **variable** is a letter or symbol that represents a number.

   An **expression** is a phrase that uses operations with numbers and variables.

   For example, $a + 3$ is an expression with the variable "a" in it.

   The variable $a$ represents any number.

   The expression $a + 3$ means 3 more than a number.

2. Write an expression for each student's age. The first one is done for you.

   a) Jolie is 5 years older than her brother.
      $b + 5$

   b) Tyler is 1 year older than his sister. $S + 1$

   c) Beth is 10 years older than her sister. $S + 10$

   d) Matthew is 2 years younger than his brother. $b + 2$

3. What does each expression mean?

   a) $b + 1$ _____    c) $m - 5$ _____

   b) $p + 3$ _____    d) $10 + f$ _____

4. Rose has $15 more than Jon.

   a) Write an expression for the amount of money Rose has. Use addition. $J + 15$

   b) Write an expression for the amount of money Jon has. Use subtraction. $J - 15$

6  Nelson Math Focus 5 Workbook                Copyright © 2009 by Nelson Education Ltd.

# Chapter 1 Lesson 7: Using Equations to Solve Problems

**GOAL**

Use equations to represent and solve problems.

1. Solve each equation. Check your answer.

   a) $p + 2 = 3$ _____

   Check: _____

   b) $b + 5 = 8$ _____

   Check: _____

   c) $s - 1 = 4$ _____

   Check: _____

   d) $4 + m = 10$ _____

   Check: _____

**At-Home Help**

An **equation** is a mathematical sentence in which the value on the left side is the same as the value on the right side.

To solve an equation like $a + 3 = 5$, you need to figure out the value of the variable. The equation says that 3 more than a number is 5, so the number must be 2.

You can also subtract 3 from 5 to calculate the value of $a$.

$5 - 3 = 2$, so $a = 2$

Check: $2 + 3 = 5$

2. Matthew is 3 years older than his brother.

   a) Write an expression for Matthew's age. _____

   b) Matthew is 10 years old. Write an equation that compares Matthew's age with his brother's age. _____

   c) Solve the equation to calculate the age of Matthew's brother.

   _____

3. Justine has some money. Her mother gave her $4 more. Now Justine has $16. How much money did Justine start with? Use an equation.

4. Nadia baked 12 cookies. She ate some of the cookies. Now she has 7 cookies left. How many cookies did Nadia eat? Use an equation.

# Chapter 1 Lesson 8: Creating Problems

**GOAL**

Create and solve problems for given equations.

1. Sydney wrote a problem for the equation $7 + a = 15$:
   *Rachel has $7. She earned $15 more.*
   *How much money does she have now?*

   **a)** What is wrong with Sydney's problem? _____

   _____

   **b)** Fix Sydney's problem so it matches the equation. _____

   _____

   **c)** Solve the problem. Check your answer.

2. Use the information to write a problem that matches the equation.

   **a)** Brandon ate more grapes than Matthew. Equation: $m + 9 = 13$
   Problem: _____

   _____

   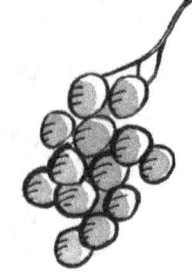

   **b)** Maya is younger than her sister. Equation: $s - 4 = 11$
   Problem: _____

   _____

3. Solve the problems in Question 2. Check your answers.

   **a)**                                              **b)**

8  *Nelson Math Focus 5 Workbook*

# Chapter 1     Test Yourself

**Circle the correct answer.**

1. What is the pattern rule for the number of circles?

    A. Start at 1 and add 3 each time.

    B. Start at 4 and add 1 each time.

    C. Start at 4 and add 2 each time.

    D. Start at 0 and add 4 each time.

    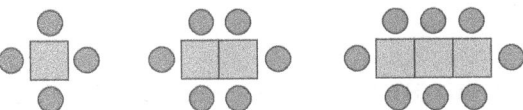

2. How much sugar is needed to make three cakes?

    | Number of cakes | Flour (mL) | Eggs | Milk (mL) | Sugar (mL) | Oil (mL) |
    |---|---|---|---|---|---|
    | 1 | 500 | 2 | 200 | 300 | 50 |
    |   |     |   |     |     |    |
    |   |     |   |     |     |    |

    A. 900 mL     B. 600 mL     C. 300 mL     D. 100 mL

3. How much flour is needed to make three cakes?

    A. 500 mL     B. 750 mL     C. 1000 mL     D. 1500 mL

4. Maya had 25 prizes. She gave 5 prizes to each student: 25, 20, 15, ... Maya gave away all her prizes. How many students were there?

    A. 3 students     B. 4 students     C. 5 students     D. 6 students

5. What is the sum of the numbers in this pattern: 3, 6, 9, 12, 15, 18?

    A. 21     B. 63     C. 42     D. 76

6. Owen worked 12 minutes more than Rachel did. Which expression represents the amount of time Owen worked?

    A. $r + 12$     B. $r - 12$     C. $12 - r$     D. $r + 12 + 12$

7. Solve the equation $p - 7 = 3$.

    A. $p = 7$     B. $p = 3$     C. $p = 4$     D. $p = 10$

8. Solve the equation $8 + n = 15$.

    A. $n = 23$     B. $n = 7$     C. $n = 8$     D. $n = 15$

# Chapter 2
## Lesson 1: Representing Numbers

**GOAL**

Represent numbers to one million using a place value chart, numerals, and words.

1. Brandon modelled a number on a place value chart. Write the standard form of his number.
   _____

   | Thousands | | | Ones | | |
   |---|---|---|---|---|---|
   | Hundreds | Tens | Ones | Hundreds | Tens | Ones |
   | ●● | ●●●●●● | ●●●●● | ●●● | ●●●●● | ● |

**At-Home Help**

**Standard form** is the way that numbers are usually written. Here are two numbers in standard form:
- 492 151 (four hundred ninety-two thousand one hundred fifty-one)
- 23 805 (twenty-three thousand eight hundred five)

2. Model 143 220 on the place value chart.

   | Thousands | | | Ones | | |
   |---|---|---|---|---|---|
   | Hundreds | Tens | Ones | Hundreds | Tens | Ones |
   |  |  |  |  |  |  |

3. Write each number in standard form.

   a) six hundred seventeen thousand one hundred twenty-six _____

   b) nine hundred one thousand three hundred twelve _____

   c) seven hundred twenty-two thousand five _____

4. Write this number in standard form and in words.

   | Thousands | | | Ones | | |
   |---|---|---|---|---|---|
   | Hundreds | Tens | Ones | Hundreds | Tens | Ones |
   | ● |  | ●●●●● | ●● |  |  |

   Words: _____

   Standard form: _____

# Chapter 2 Lesson 2

## Using Expanded Form

**GOAL**

Represent, describe, and compare numbers to one million.

1. Write the number 863 291 in expanded form.

   ____ hundred thousands + ____ ten thousands
   + ____ thousands + ____ hundreds
   + ____ tens + ____ one

2. Write the number 582 100 in expanded form using numerals.

   582 100  _500 000 +_ _____

3. Write each number in standard form.

   a) 1 hundred thousand + 2 ten thousands
      + 5 thousands + 7 hundreds + 8 tens + 2 ones _____

   b) 50 000 + 3000 + 200 + 60 + 9 _____

   c) 500 000 + 30 000 + 5000 + 100 + 90 + 2 _____

   d) 700 000 + 10 000 + 800 + 40 + 3 _____

4. Write the numbers in Question 3 in order from greatest to least.

   _____

5. Draw seven counters on the place value chart to make a six-digit number. Write the standard form and the expanded form of your number.

   Standard form: _____

   Expanded form: _____

**At-Home Help**

Expanded form is a way to write a number that shows the value of each digit. For example, the expanded form of 193 245 is:
1 hundred thousand
+ 9 ten thousands
+ 3 thousands + 2 hundreds
+ 4 tens + 5 ones, OR
100 000 + 90 000 + 3000 + 200 + 40 + 5.

| Thousands | | | Ones | | |
|---|---|---|---|---|---|
| Hundreds | Tens | Ones | Hundreds | Tens | Ones |
|  |  |  |  |  |  |

# Chapter 2
# Lesson 3
# Renaming Numbers

**GOAL**

Rename numbers that have up to seven digits.

1. Mateo, Jolie, and Tyler are playing a game. Each student has play money. They can use the money to buy decorated tiles.
   Mateo has $387 622.
   Jolie has $186 200.
   Tyler has $420 331.

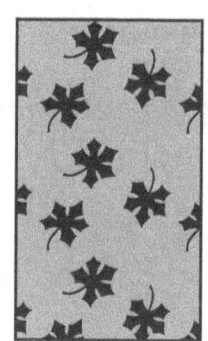
leaves
$100 000

flowers
$10 000

triangles
$1000

stripes
$100

dots
$10

plain
$1

   a) Which student has the most play money? **Tyler**

   b) How many leaf tiles can Mateo buy? **3**

   c) Jolie says that she can buy 18 flower tiles.
      Is she correct? Explain.
      **yes she is corect**

   d) Tyler says, "I can buy 42 flower tiles and 331 plain tiles."
      Write two other sets of tiles that Tyler can buy with his money.
      **dots stripes**

   e) Write three different sets of tiles that Mateo can buy.

# Chapter 2 Lesson 4: Rounding Numbers

**GOAL**

Round numbers to the nearest hundred thousand, the nearest ten thousand, and the nearest thousand.

**At-Home Help**

You can round 486 186 in different ways:
- to the nearest hundred thousand: 500 000
- to the nearest ten thousand: 490 000
- to the nearest thousand: 486 000

1. Mark each number on the number line. Then round each number to the nearest hundred thousand.

   a) 215 000  __215 000__

   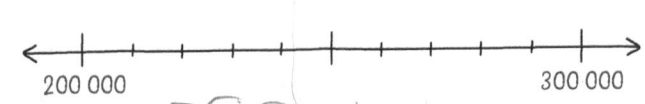
   200 000        300 000

   b) 557 000  __560 000__

   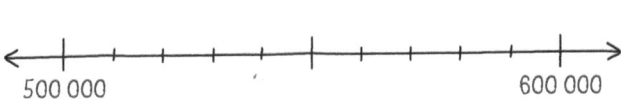
   500 000        600 000

2. Is 863 371 closer to 800 000 or 900 000? How do you know?
   
   863 371 is not color because we need to rond to 900 000.

3. Round each number to the nearest ten thousand.
   
   a) 741 938 __800 000__    c) 578 000 __500 000__
   
   b) 116 220 __100 000__    d) 386 442 __200 000__

4. Round each number to the nearest thousand.
   
   a) 561 372 __500 000__    c) 983 871 __1000 000__
   
   b) 110 283 __100 000__    d) 453 666 __300 000__

5. Round 736 927 to the nearest hundred thousand, ten thousand, and thousand.

# Chapter 2 Lesson 5: Exploring One Million

**GOAL**

Describe one million in various ways.

Tyler collects pennies. He wants to know how many pennies he needs to collect to have $10, $100, $1000, and $10 000.

1. How many pennies are in $1?
   __100__ pennies in $1

2. How many pennies are in $10?
   __10 00__ hundreds = _____ pennies in $10

3. How many pennies are in $100?
   __100 000__ hundreds = _____ pennies in $100

4. How many pennies are in $1000?
   __1000 000__ hundreds = _____ pennies in $1000

5. What pattern do you notice in the number of pennies?
   __On zero is add__

6. How many pennies are in $10 000?
   __10000 000__ pennies in $10 000

7. It takes Tyler 1 month to collect 100 pennies.
   How many months would it take him to collect $1? __1__
   How many months would it take him to collect $10 000 worth of pennies? Explain your thinking.

   _____

# Chapter 2 Lesson 6: Decimal Place Value

**GOAL**

Read, write, and model decimals.

1. Write each number in standard form.

    a) 1 + 0.3 + 0.02 + 0.007 _____

    b) 6 + 0.4 + 0.009 _____

    c) 0.5 + 0.03 + 0.005 _____

2. Write each number in expanded form using numerals.

    a) 3.573 _____

    b) 0.486 _____

    c) 1.081 _____

3. Write each number in words. The first one is done for you.

    a) 1.522  one and five hundred twenty-two thousandths

    b) 4.112 _____

    c) 0.703 _____

    d) 0.008 _____

4. Owen modelled a decimal using base ten blocks on a place value chart. What is Owen's decimal?

    _____

### At-Home Help

You can use base ten blocks to model decimal values.

- one block, or 1
- one tenth of a block, or 0.1
- one hundredth of a block, or 0.01
- one thousandth of a block, or 0.001

To read a number with a decimal, say "and" for the decimal part. Omit the "and" if there is no whole number part. For example:

- 1.382 is one and three hundred eighty-two thousandths.
- 0.047 is forty-seven thousandths.

| Thousands | | | Ones | | |
|---|---|---|---|---|---|
| Hundreds | Tens | Ones | Tenths | Hundredths | Thousandths |
|  |  | 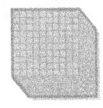 |  | ▌▌ | 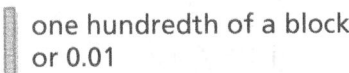 |

# Chapter 2 Lesson 7: Renaming Decimals

**GOAL**

Represent decimals and relate them to fractions.

1. There are 1000 cans of drinks.
   350 of the cans hold juice.

   **a)** Colour the thousandths grid to represent the number of juice cans.

   **At-Home Help**

   Equivalent means having the same value. For example:
   - 0.4, 0.40, and 0.400 are equivalent decimals.
   - $\frac{3}{10}$, $\frac{30}{100}$, and $\frac{300}{1000}$ are equivalent fractions.
   - 0.08 is equivalent to 0.080, or $\frac{8}{100}$, or $\frac{80}{1000}$.

   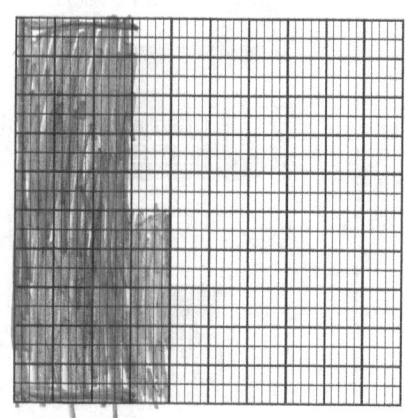

   **b)** Complete these fractions to show the number of juice cans. $\frac{35}{100}$ or $\frac{350}{1000}$

   **c)** Write the number of juice cans as a decimal hundredth. _____

   **d)** Write the number of juice cans as a decimal thousandth. _____

2. Write each decimal as a decimal hundredth and as a decimal thousandth.

   **a)** 0.4  __0.40__ and _____   **c)** 0.9 _____ and _____

   **b)** 0.1 _____ and _____   **d)** 0.7 _____ and _____

3. Write each fraction as a decimal thousandth and as a decimal hundredth.

   **a)** $\frac{730}{1000}$ _____ and _____   **c)** $\frac{80}{1000}$ _____ and _____

   **b)** $\frac{120}{1000}$ _____ and _____   **d)** $\frac{10}{1000}$ _____ and _____

# Chapter 2 Lesson 8: Communicating about Equivalent Decimals

**GOAL**

Explain whether two decimals are equivalent.

1. Explain how you know that 0.6 is equivalent to 0.60. Use the Communication Checklist.

   _____
   _____
   _____

   **At-Home Help**

   **Communication Checklist**
   - ✔ Did you use math language?
   - ✔ Did you include the right amount of detail?
   - ✔ Did you include a diagram?

2. Brandon lives 100 m away from the school. He says, "I walked 50 m. This means that I walked 0.05 of the distance." Do you agree with Brandon? Explain why or why not.

   *he wakt hat way*

3. Jay's home is 100 m away from the school. He walked 0.6 of the distance. How many metres did he walk? How do you know?

   *60 ot of 100    60/100*

4. Rachel's home is 1000 m away from the school. She walked 0.8 of the distance. How many metres did she walk? How do you know?

   *80 parts of the way*

# Chapter 2
# Lesson 9
# Rounding Decimals

**GOAL**

Interpret rounded decimals, and round decimals to the nearest tenth or the nearest hundredth.

1. Round each decimal to the nearest hundredth. Use the number line to help you.

   a) 0.239 _____    c) 0.224 _____
   b) 0.213 _____    d) 0.207 _____

**At-Home Help**

You can round decimals to the nearest hundredth or to the nearest tenth.

For example, round 0.574 to the nearest hundredth and tenth.
- nearest hundredth: 0.57
- nearest tenth: 0.6

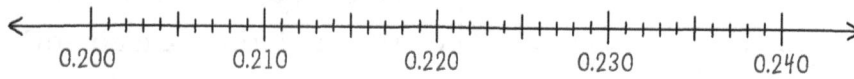

2. Round each decimal to the nearest tenth. Use the number line to help you.

   a) 0.420 _____    c) 0.385 _____
   b) 0.570 _____    d) 0.612 _____

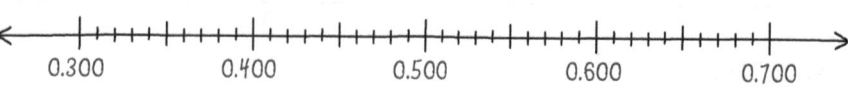

3. Taylor surveyed 1000 students at her school. These are her results:
   - 549 students have cats
   - 304 students have dogs
   - 118 students have fish

   a) Out of 100 students, about how many have cats? about _____ students
   b) Out of 100 students, about how many have dogs? about _____ students
   c) Out of 100 students, about how many have fish? about _____ students

4. Circle the numbers that round to 2.78 if you are rounding to the nearest hundredth.

   2.783    2.787    2.778    2.786    2.773    2.777

**Chapter 2 Lesson 10**

# Comparing and Ordering Decimals

**GOAL**

Compare and order decimals up to decimal thousandths.

1. Jolie's lunch cost $3.22. Sydney's lunch cost $4.21. Mateo's lunch cost $3.76.

    a) Which lunch cost the most? __Sydney's__

    b) Which lunch cost the least? __jolies__

    c) Put the lunch costs in order from least cost to greatest cost.

    _____

    **At-Home Help**

    Here are some ways to compare and order decimals:
    - Use a place value chart.
    - Use a number line.
    - Use a thousandths grid.

2. Compare each pair of numbers using <, >, or =.

    a) 4.0 > 0.4        c) 5.3 < 6.8        e) 6.72 > 6.027
    b) 0.20 > 0.2       d) 0.45 > 0.29      f) 1.515 < 5.105

3. Order each set of numbers from greatest to least.

    a) 5.68, 3.02, 6.33, 8.21, 4.99  __3.02, 4.99, 5.68, 6.33, 8.21__

    b) 0.831, 3.23, 0.996, 0.5, 1.005  _____

    c) 0.090, 0.281, 0.300, 0.007, 0.111  _____

4. Jolie ran 0.074 km, Tyler ran 0.114 km, and Rachel ran 0.099 km. Who ran the shortest distance? Who ran the farthest?

    _____

5. Sam, Brandon, Sydney, and Rachel made towers of bricks. They measured the heights of their towers. Put the tower heights in order from least to greatest.

    **Height of Towers**

    | Student | Height (m) |
    |---------|------------|
    | Rachel  | 0.729      |
    | Sam     | 1.730      |
    | Brandon | 0.972      |
    | Sydney  | 1.400      |

Copyright © 2009 by Nelson Education Ltd.

# Chapter 2    Test Yourself

**Circle the correct answer.**

1. What number is represented on the place value chart?

   | Thousands | | | Ones | | |
   |---|---|---|---|---|---|
   | Hundreds | Tens | Ones | Hundreds | Tens | Ones |
   | 2 | | 5 | 1 | 1 | 5 |

   **A.** 203 115    **C.** two hundred five thousand one hundred fifteen
   **B.** 250 150    **D.** two hundred fifty thousand one hundred fifteen

2. Which number is greatest?

   **A.** 800 000 + 60 000    **C.** 800 000 + 60 000 + 30
   **B.** 800 000 + 6 000 + 300    **D.** They all have the same value.

3. Jolie rounded a number to the nearest hundred thousand, ten thousand, and thousand. She got 700 000, 720 000, and 719 000. Which number could Jolie have started with?

   **A.** 719 201    **B.** 720 201    **C.** 719 701    **D.** 720 701

4. What is the standard form of the number 7 + 0.4 + 0.06 + 0.001?

   **A.** 7.4061    **B.** 7.461    **C.** 7.4601    **D.** 74.06001

5. What is the equivalent decimal hundredth and decimal thousandth of 0.8?

   **A.** 0.08 and 0.008    **C.** 800 and 8 000
   **B.** 0.88 and 0.888    **D.** 0.80 and 0.800

6. Which pair of numbers round to the same hundredth?

   **A.** 0.680 and 0.699    **C.** 0.582 and 0.679
   **B.** 0.680 and 0.679    **D.** 0.699 and 0.582

7. Which comparison is not true?

   **A.** 0.090 < 0.900    **B.** 1.6 > 2.5    **C.** 1.92 > 0.92    **D.** 0.284 > 0.274

# Chapter 3 Lesson 1

# Estimating Whole-Number Sums and Differences

**GOAL**

Estimate sums and differences to solve problems.

1. Estimate each sum. Show the numbers you used.

   a) 41 008 + 29 100 is about
   
   60 108
   
   b) 8 726 + 1 974 is about
   
   9 500
   
   c) 301 040 + 512 113 is about
   
   913 163

2. Estimate each difference.

   a) 18 015 − 2 632 is about
   
   35347
   
   b) 9 499 − 3 999 is about
   
   12 588
   
   c) 700 988 − 501 012 is about
   
   110 979

**At-Home Help**

To estimate sums and differences, use nearby numbers that are easy to work with. For example:

Estimate 18 948 − 2 085.

18 948 is about 19 000.
2 085 is about 2 000.
19 000 − 2 000 = 17 000

OR

18 948 is about 18 900.
2 085 is about 2 100.
18 900 − 2 100 = 16 800

3. A weather balloon was sent up into the atmosphere. First, it rose to 48 700 m. Then it dropped down to 18 980 m. About how many metres did it drop?

4. 297 021 adults and 321 514 children live in Lakeview. About how many people live in Lakeview?

# Chapter 3 Lesson 2: Communicating about Estimating and Calculating

**GOAL**

Explain clearly how to estimate and calculate.

1. Tyler estimated the total number of students.

    **Students at Lakeview Junior School**

    | Grade | Number of students |
    |---|---|
    | Kindergarten and Grade 1 | 792 |
    | Grades 2 and 3 | 1046 |
    | Grades 4 and 5 | 3217 |

    **At-Home Help**

    **Communication Checklist**
    - ✔ Did you explain your thinking?
    - ✔ Did you show all the steps?
    - ✔ Did you use math language?

    Tyler's solution and explanation:

    I can solve the problem by figuring out out how many students there are. The first two numbers are both about 1000. All the numbers together are about 5000.

    a) How can Tyler improve his explanation?  792 + 1046 + 3217 = 2055

    b) Write a new solution and explanation. Use the Communication Checklist.

    _____
    _____
    _____
    _____

2. About how many trees are in Lakeview Forest? Use the Communication Checklist.

    About 72250

    **Trees in Lakeview Forest**

    | Kind of tree | Number of trees |
    |---|---|
    | pine | 286 215 |
    | oak | 109 283 |
    | maple | 327 003 |

# Chapter 3 Lesson 3
# Estimating Decimal Sums and Differences

**GOAL**

Estimate sums and differences with decimals.

1. Estimate each sum.
   a) 0.32 + 0.28 is about __0.60__
   b) 0.099 + 0.410 is about __0.509__
   c) 1.03 + 2.61 is about __3.64__

2. Estimate each difference.
   a) 1.99 − 1 is about __0.97__
   b) 0.821 − 0.490 is about __0.312__
   c) 3.97 − 0.77 is about __4.75__

**At-Home Help**

To estimate sums and differences, use nearby numbers that are easy to work with. For example:
Estimate 0.685 + 0.199.
0.685 is about 0.7.
0.199 is about 0.2.
0.7 + 0.2 = 0.9
So 0.685 + 0.199 is about 0.9.

3. Estimate to match the sums and differences with the correct answers.

   0.713 − 0.522        2.02
   4.80 − 0.32          0.631
   0.229 + 0.402        0.066
   0.047 + 0.019        0.801
   2.99 − 0.97          4.48
   0.062 + 0.739        0.191

4. Rebecca's bedroom walls have an area of 17.29 square metres. She has enough yellow paint to cover 11.88 square metres. She has enough white paint to cover 5.11 square metres. Does Rebecca have enough paint to colour her bedroom yellow and white?

   no  16.99

# Chapter 3 Lesson 4: Adding Decimals Using Mental Math

**GOAL**

Solve problems by using mental math to add decimals.

1. Add using mental math.
   a) 0.49 + 1.51  _2.000_
   b) 0.99 + 0.11  _1.100_
   c) 0.001 + 0.099  _0.100_
   d) 1.010 + 1.090  _2.100_

2. Add using mental math.
   a) 2.999 + 0.054  _3.053_
   b) 0.847 + 5.999  _6.846_
   c) 4.001 + 0.973  _4.974_
   d) 3.498 + 2.002  _5.500_

**At-Home Help**

Here is one way to add decimals using mental math:

Add (or subtract) a little bit to one number to round it. Then subtract (or add) the same amount from the other number.

For example, add 2.99 + 0.73. Add 0.01 to the first number to get 3. Subtract 0.01 from the second number to get 0.72. 3.00 + 0.72 = 3.72

3. Ami went for a walk around the park.

   a) How far did Ami walk? Show your work.

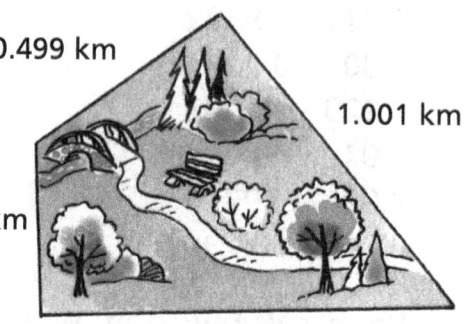

0.499 km
1.001 km
0.251 km
0.999 km

   b) Use estimating to check your answer. Show your work.

# Adding Decimals by Regrouping

## GOAL
Solve problems by adding decimals.

1. Calculate.

   a)  0.039
       + 0.153
       *0.192*

   b)  0.875
       + 0.125
       *1.000*

   c)  1.522
       + 0.180
       *1.702*

   d)  5.423
       + 2.627
       *8.050*

2. Tyler added 1.228 + 0.457 like this:
   1.228 + 0.400 = 1.628
   1.628 + 0.050 = 1.678
   1.678 + 0.007 = 1.685

   a) Use Tyler's method to add 0.944 + 0.045. Show your work. *.989*

   b) Use Tyler's method to add 4.283 + 0.164. Show your work. *4.447*

**At-Home Help**

Here is one way to add decimals:

**Step 1:** Line up digits with the same place value.

**Step 2:** Add the thousandths, then hundredths, then tenths, then ones.

**Step 3:** If any sum is more than 10, regroup.

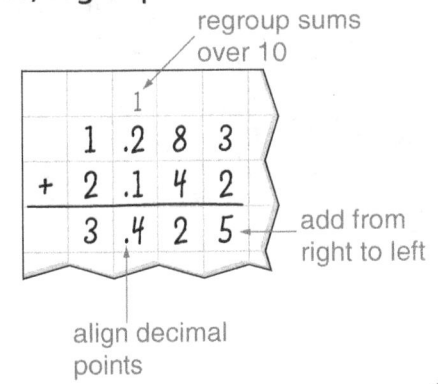

3. Calculate. Choose your own method.

   a) 0.412 + 1.388
      *1.800*

   b) 2.871 + 3.006
      *5.877*

   c) 1.862 + 3.501
      *5.026*

# Chapter 3 Lesson 6: Exploring Problems that Involve Decimals

**GOAL**

Use your own strategies to solve a problem that involves adding and subtracting decimals.

Ami has $20.00. She bought a pencil case for $6.29.
She wants to buy three more things.
Which things can she buy?
Give Ami two choices. Show your work.

```
 1 1 1
  4 9 9
+ 6 2 9
-------
1 1 2 8
```

$859

answer
```
   1
  1 1 2 8
  +  8 5 9
  --------
  1 1 9 8 7
```

# Subtracting Decimals by Regrouping

**GOAL**

Regroup to solve subtraction problems.

1. Maya used regrouping to subtract.

   a) How did Maya regroup 1.724 to get 1 one, 6 tenths, 12 hundredths, and 4 thousandths?

   ```
       1  6 12  4
       1 . 7  2  4
     - 0 . 5  8  3
       _____
       1 . 1  4  1
   ```

   _____
   _____
   _____

   b) Complete Maya's subtraction.

2. Calculate.

   a)  0.82
      − 0.26
      _____
       0.56

   b)  2.07
      − 1.95
      _____
       0.12

   c)  2.405
      − 0.500
      _____
       1.905

   d)  5.000
      − 0.226
      _____

**At-Home Help**

You can regroup decimals to help you subtract. For example, subtract 5.275 − 2.338.

Regroup 5.275 to make the subtraction easier.

Regroup 5 ones and 2 tenths as 4 ones and 12 tenths.

Regroup 7 hundredths and 5 thousandths as 6 hundredths and 15 thousandths.

```
    4 12  6 15
    5 . 2  7  5
  - 2 . 3  3  8
    _____
    2 . 9  3  7
```

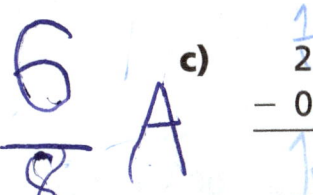

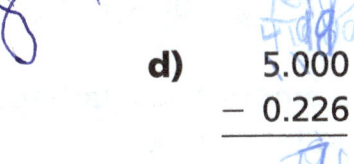

3. Rebecca hiked 2.062 km of a 4.500 km hike. How much of the hike is left?

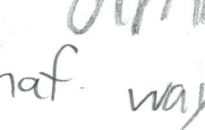

Chapter 3: Adding and Subtracting Decimals

# Chapter 3 Lesson 8: Subtracting Decimals by Renaming

**GOAL**

Rename decimals to make subtraction easier.

1. Jay wants to calculate 9 − 0.46. How can he rename the 9 to help him subtract?

   _____

2. Calculate by renaming. Show your work.

   a) 5.0 − 0.2

   b) 9 − 0.08

   c) 3 − 0.472

   d) 1 − 0.721

   e) 6.000 − 3.625

**At-Home Help**

You can rename decimals to help you subtract. For example, 5 − 0.743.

First, rename 5 as 4.999 + 0.001.

   4.999 + 0.001
   ~~5.000~~
   − 0.743
   4.256 + 0.001 = 4.257

3. Owen, Sydney, and Jolie are collecting 4.00 kg of garbage each for Earth Day.
   So far, they have collected these amounts of garbage:
   Owen 0.72 kg, Sydney 3.02 kg, Jolie 2.145 kg.
   How much more does each student need to collect?

   Owen:          Sydney:          Jolie:

28  Nelson Math Focus 5 Workbook

# Chapter 3   Test Yourself

**Circle the correct answer.**

1. Estimate to choose the correct answer for 10 362 + 28 364.
   A. 29 676    **B. 38 726**    C. 45 696    D. 59 019

2. Which number is a good estimate for the sum 498 + 1066 + 3512?
   A. 2000    B. 3000    C. 4000    **D. 5000**

3. Estimate to choose the correct answer for 1.08 + 0.66.
   **A. 1.74**    B. 0.74    C. 2.74    D. 7.4

4. Estimate to choose the correct answer for 0.975 − 0.222.
   A. 75.3    B. 7.53    **C. 0.753**    D. 0.0753

5. Calculate 0.34 + 0.11.
   A. 0.23    **B. 0.45**    C. 0.83    D. 0.51

6. Calculate 2.82 + 5.17.
   A. 3.72    B. 8.11    **C. 7.99**    D. 6.125

7. Calculate 0.283 + 1.347.
   **A. 1.630**    B. 1.072    C. 3.000    D. 1.520

8. Calculate 0.882 + 0.442.
   A. 2.413    B. 4.231    C. 3.124    **D. 1.324**

9. Estimate to choose the correct answer for 4.82 − 1.77.
   **A. 0.305**    B. 3.05    C. 30.5    D. 305

10. Calculate 0.812 − 0.471.
    **A. 0.341**    B. 0.421    C. 0.881    D. 0.651

11. Calculate 7 − 0.436.
    A. 6.722    B. 5.832    C. 6.564    **D. 7.129**

# Chapter 4
## Lesson 1: Exploring Types of Data

**GOAL**

Tell the difference between first-hand data and second-hand data.

1. Identify each type of data as first-hand data or second-hand data.

    a) data that you find on the Internet

    _____

    b) data that you get from asking friends

    _____

> **At-Home Help**
>
> **First-hand data** is information that you collect yourself. For example, if you conduct a survey among your classmates, you will get first-hand data.
>
> **Second-hand data** is information that others have collected. For example, if you get information from a newspaper, it is second-hand data.

2. Lauren wants to know which countries people in Canada tend to visit the most.

    a) How could Lauren get first-hand data on this topic?

    _____

    b) How could she get second-hand data on this topic?

    _____

3. Ask 10 Canadians which other country they have visited the most. Fill in the chart.

    a) Compare your chart with the chart below it. Which chart is first-hand data? Which is second-hand data?

    _____

    _____

    b) Do the first-hand data give you the same results as the second-hand data? Explain your thinking.

    _____

**Country Visited the Most**

| Country | Number of people |
|---|---|
|  |  |
|  |  |
|  |  |

**Country Visited the Most**

| Country | Number of people |
|---|---|
| United States | 9.0 million |
| U.K. | 2.0 million |
| France | 1.5 million |
| Mexico | 1.0 million |

# Chapter 4 Lesson 2: Using First-Hand Data

**GOAL**

Create and answer questions using first-hand data.

1. Circle the question(s) you would answer using first-hand data.

    A. How many people are in Canada?

    B. How many people are in your class?

    C. How many people in your grade have pets?

    D. How many people in Calgary own cars?

    **At-Home Help**

    Here are some ways to collect first-hand data:
    - do interviews
    - do a survey
    - do an experiment
    - observe

2. How would you collect first-hand data to answer each question? Explain your choice.

    a) What flavour of ice cream should you buy for the class party?

    _____

    _____

    b) If you flip a coin four times, how many times will you get heads?

    _____

3. a) Write a question you could ask your friends and family about their favourite food. Give them some choices to choose from.

    _____

    b) Why can this question be answered using first-hand data?

    _____

    c) What method could you use to collect the data?

    _____

    d) Collect the data, and answer your question.

    _____

    _____

# Chapter 4
## Lesson 3: Using Second-Hand Data

**GOAL**

Create questions that can be answered using second-hand data.

**At-Home Help**

Here are some ways to collect second-hand data:
- search the Internet
- read a book
- look in newspapers or magazines
- ask an expert

1. **a)** Many different types of birds live in Canada. Write a question about birds that you can answer using first-hand data.

   _____

   _____

   **b)** How could you collect data to answer your question?

   _____

2. **a)** Write a question about birds that you can answer using second-hand data.

   _____

   **b)** Why can you answer the question using second-hand data?

   _____

   **c)** How could you collect data to answer your question?

   _____

   **d)** Collect the data, and answer your question.

   _____

3. Write a question about birds that you can answer using the given data.

   _____

   _____

| Bird | Number of days to learn how to fly |
| --- | --- |
| Cardinal | 10 |
| Blue jay | 21 |
| Chickadee | 16 |

# Chapter 4 Lesson 4: Interpreting Double-Bar Graphs

**GOAL**

Interpret and compare double-bar graphs.

1. Desmond and Jay used a double-bar graph to compare their amounts of exercise.

   a) On which days did both boys exercise?
   _____

   b) Which boy exercised more on Thursday? _____

   c) On which day did both boys exercise the same amount? _____

   d) How many minutes did Desmond exercise on Friday? _____

   e) How many minutes did Jay exercise on Friday? _____

   **At-Home Help**

   A **double-bar graph** is a graph with pairs of bars. Each pair of bars represents two different sets of data.

   A **legend** is an explanation of the symbols or colours on a graph.

2. Sydney and Rebecca did surveys asking students about their favourite sport. Each girl graphed her data.

   a) Do their graphs show the same data? Explain.
   _____
   _____
   _____

   b) Which girl collected the most data? Explain.
   _____
   _____

Chapter 4: Data Relationships  33

# Constructing Double-Bar Graphs

**GOAL**

Construct and interpret double-bar graphs.

Two mall managers did a survey.

**Stores that Customers Visit the Most**

| Type of store | Number of people in 1 hour at Pinecrest Mall | Number of people in 1 hour at Millstreet Mall |
|---|---|---|
| shoes | 6 | 14 |
| women's fashion | 18 | 26 |
| men's fashion | 4 | 14 |
| children's fashion | 8 | 8 |
| teen fashion | 20 | 24 |

**At-Home Help**

**Communication Checklist**
Did you include these parts in your graph?
✔ Title
✔ Scale
✔ Legend
✔ Labels

**1. a)** Use the data in the chart to create a double-bar graph.

**b)** A new store is opening at Millstreet Mall. Which type of store do you think it should be? Explain your thinking.

_____

_____

34  Nelson Math Focus 5 Workbook

# Solving Problems by Creating Diagrams

**GOAL**

Use diagrams, charts, or graphs to solve problems.

The whooping crane, the blue whale, the woodland caribou, and the wolverine are all endangered animals.

**Which endangered animal do the most people know about?**

1. Write a survey question that you can ask adults and students to solve the problem.

   _____
   _____

2. Survey five adults and five students. Organize your data in the chart.

   **Endangered Animals that People Know About**

   | Endangered animal | People who know about it ||
   |---|---|---|
   |  | Adults | Students |
   |  |  |  |
   |  |  |  |
   |  |  |  |
   |  |  |  |

3. Use your data to construct a double-bar graph.

4. Which endangered animals do the most adults know about?

   _____

5. Which endangered animals do the most students know about?

   _____

# Chapter 4   Test Yourself

Circle the correct answer.

1. Which kind of information is first-hand data?

    A. information from a book

    B. data found on the Internet

    C. news from the TV

    D. your observations from an experiment

2. Which question would you answer using second-hand data?

    A. How many students are in your class?

    B. How many people in Ontario go to school?

    C. How many people on your block drive a car?

    D. What kinds of trees grow in your schoolyard?

3. Which question can be answered using the data in the chart?

    A. Which team got the most points in Game 1?

    B. Is Team 1 better than Team 2 at basketball?

    C. How many people are on each team?

    D. Did all the teams play at the same time?

    **Basketball Results**

    | Team | Game 1 | Game 2 | Game 3 |
    |------|--------|--------|--------|
    | Team 1 | 3 points | 2 points | 1 point |
    | Team 2 | 2 points | 4 points | 2 points |
    | Team 3 | 5 points | 3 points | 0 points |

4. Which two double-bar graphs show the same data?

    A. Graphs 1 and 2   B. Graphs 1 and 3   C. Graphs 3 and 4   D. Graphs 2 and 4

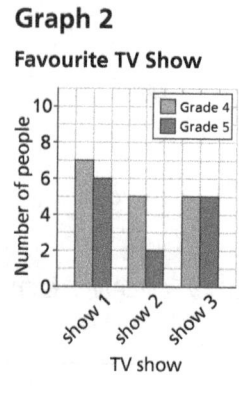
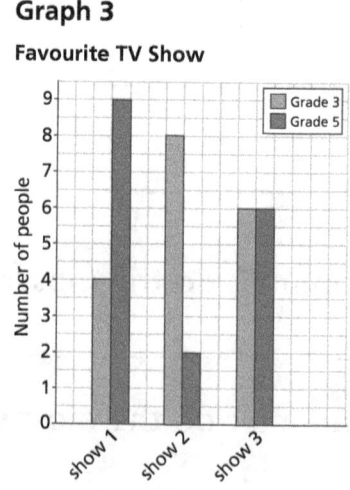
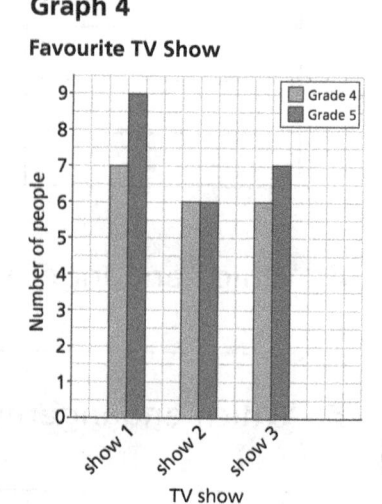

# Chapter 5 Lesson 1

# Performing Translations

**GOAL**

Perform, describe, and identify translations of 2-D shapes.

1. Brandon moved shape A to shape B. What translation rule did he use?

   _____
   _____

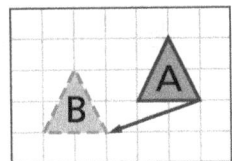

**At-Home Help**

A **translation** is the result of sliding a shape along a straight line.

A **translation rule** is a way of describing a translation with pictures or numbers. For example, "I translated the rectangle five units right and two units up. I used the black slide arrow."

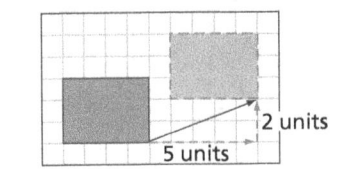

2. Which shape is a translation of shape C?

   _____

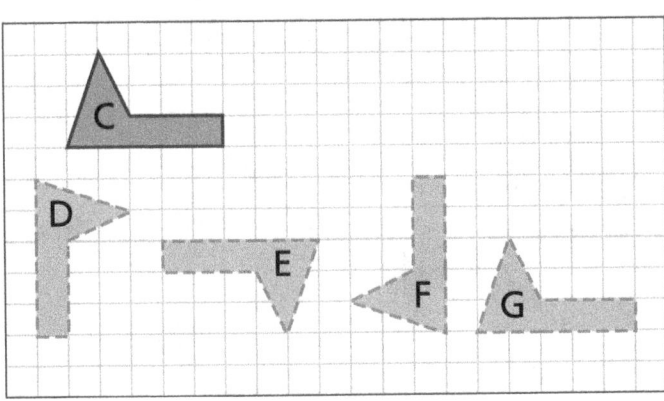

3. a) Translate rectangle M to a new position. Sketch the new shape.

   b) Describe the translation rule you used.

   _____
   _____

   c) Translate rectangle M five units to the right. Sketch the new shape.

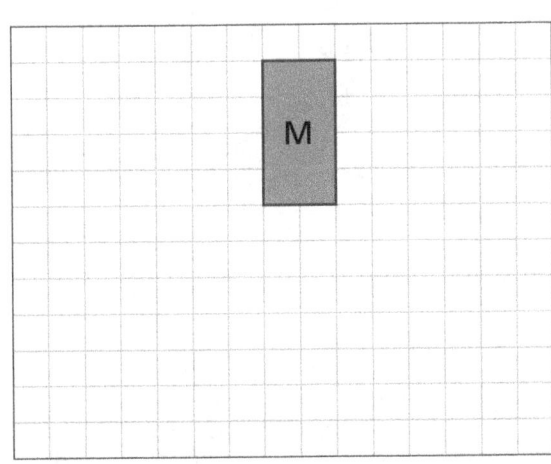

Chapter 5: Motion Geometry

# Chapter 5 Lesson 2: Exploring Reflections Using a Mirror

**GOAL**

Perform and identify reflections of shapes.

You will need a transparent mirror and a ruler.

You can create different designs by drawing the reflection of a shape.

1. For each shape below, draw a line of reflection. Then sketch the reflection to create a design.

### At-Home Help

A **reflection** is the result of flipping a 2-D shape across a line of reflection.

A **line of reflection** is a line that falls exactly halfway between the points of a shape and the matching points of its reflection. For example:

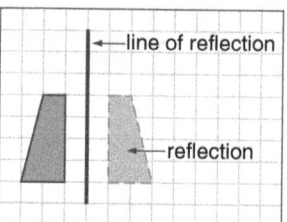

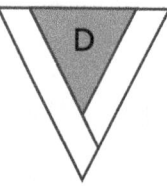

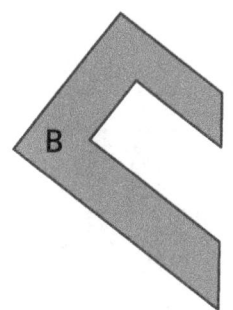

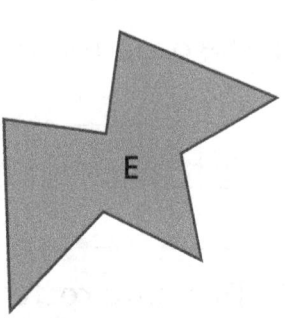

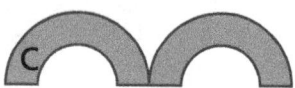

38   Nelson Math Focus 5 Workbook

Copyright © 2009 by Nelson Education Ltd.

# Performing Reflections on a Grid

**GOAL**

Reflect shapes on a grid, and describe their positions and orientation.

1. Reflect each shape across the black line of reflection. Sketch the reflection.

   a)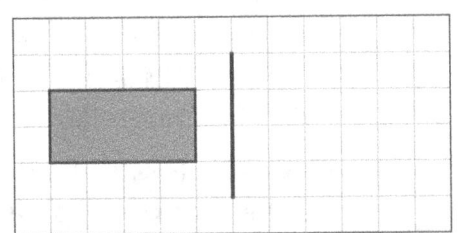
   
   b)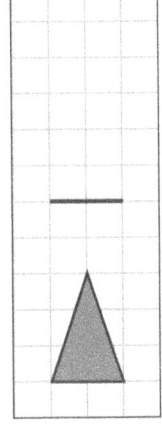

**At-Home Help**

To reflect a shape on a grid, count the number of units from the line of reflection to each vertex.

In this example, the line of reflection is five units from A, three units from B, one unit from C, and three units from D.

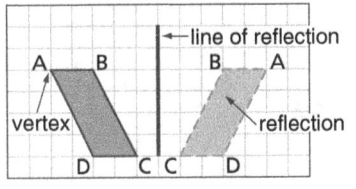

2. For each shape, draw a line of reflection. Then reflect and sketch the new shape.

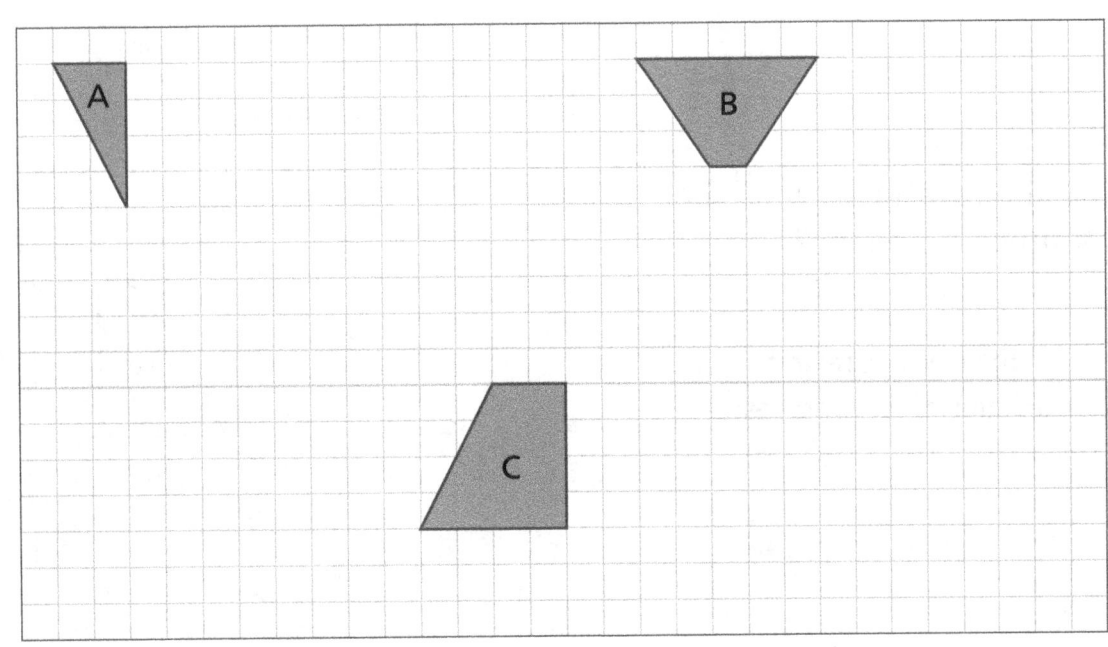

Copyright © 2009 by Nelson Education Ltd.    Chapter 5: Motion Geometry   **39**

# Chapter 5
## Lesson 4 — Performing Rotations

**GOAL**

Perform, describe, and identify rotations of shapes.

1. For each rotation, identify the amount ($\frac{1}{4}$ turn, $\frac{1}{2}$ turn, or $\frac{3}{4}$ turn) and the direction (cw or ccw).

   a)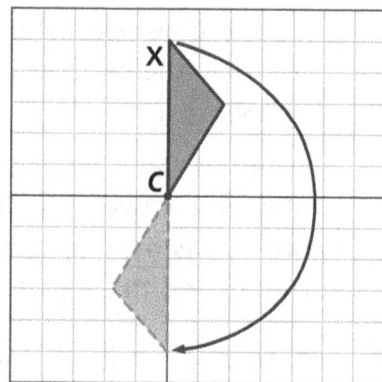

   amount
   _____

   direction
   _____

   b)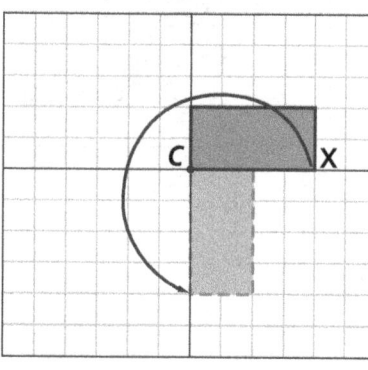

   amount
   _____

   direction
   _____

**At-Home Help**

A **rotation** is the result of turning a shape. The **centre of rotation** is the point that a shape turns around.

**Clockwise (cw)** is the direction in which a clock's hands move. **Counter-clockwise (ccw)** is the opposite direction to clockwise.

You can rotate a shape a $\frac{1}{4}$ turn, a $\frac{1}{2}$ turn, or a $\frac{3}{4}$ turn in either direction. For example:

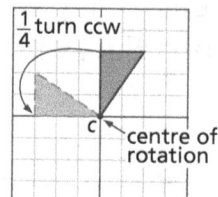
centre of rotation

2. a) Identify the rotation from shape 1 to shape 2.

   _____

   b) Identify a different rotation that would give the same result.

   _____

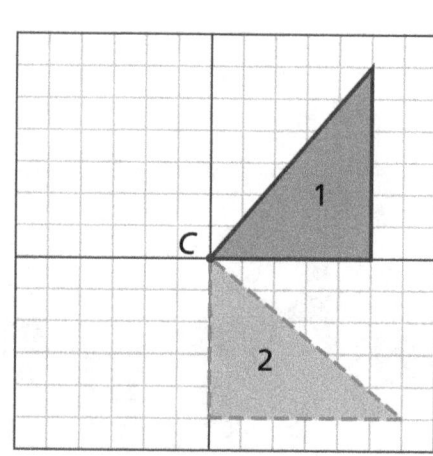

# Communicating about Transformations

**GOAL**

Describe transformations using math language.

1. Stefan described a translation. He said, "I moved the shape over and up to get the new shape."

   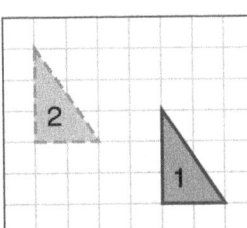

   Improve Stefan's description. Use the Communication Checklist to help you.

   _____
   _____
   _____

**At-Home Help**

A **transformation** is the result of moving a shape according to a rule to get a new image. Translations, reflections, and rotations are all examples of transformations.

Use this Communication Checklist to communicate about transformations.
- ✔ Did you use math language?
- ✔ Did you include diagrams?
- ✔ Did you show the right amount of detail?

2. Describe each transformation of shape A.

   a) shape A to shape B

   _____
   _____
   _____

   b) shape A to shape C

   _____
   _____
   _____

   c) shape A to shape D

   _____
   _____

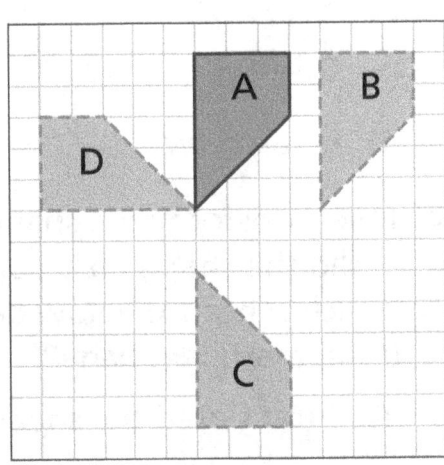

Copyright © 2009 by Nelson Education Ltd.                Chapter 5: Motion Geometry    41

# Chapter 5  Test Yourself

Circle the correct answer.

1. Which shape shows shape 1 translated three units left and four units down?

    A. shape 2
    B. shape 3
    C. shape 4
    D. shape 5

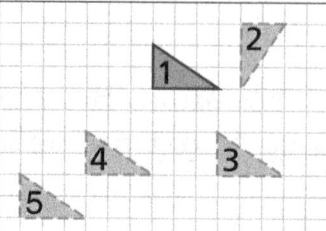

2. Which shape is a reflection of shape A?

    A. shape B
    B. shape C
    C. shape D
    D. shape E

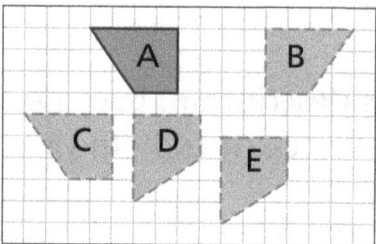

3. How is shape 1 rotated to get shape 2?

    A. $\frac{3}{4}$ turn ccw
    B. $\frac{1}{2}$ turn ccw
    C. $\frac{1}{4}$ turn cw
    D. $\frac{1}{4}$ turn ccw

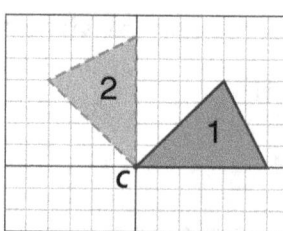

4. Jolie transformed a shape. She said, "I slid the shape down and then flipped it." Which sentence below describes Jolie's transformation using math language?

    A. I translated the shape five units down, and then reflected it.
    B. I moved the shape to the right, and then rotated it.
    C. I translated the shape three units up, and then transformed it.
    D. I rotated the shape a $\frac{1}{4}$ turn ccw, and then reflected it.

42   Nelson Math Focus 5 Workbook

# Chapter 6 Lesson 1: Multiplication Strategies

**GOAL**

Multiply one-digit numbers using mental math strategies.

1. Calculate.

   a) $3 \times 5 =$ _____  c) $8 \times 2 =$ _____

   b) $4 \times 7 =$ _____  d) $6 \times 5 =$ _____

2. Use doubling to calculate.

   a) $2 \times 4 =$ _____, so $4 \times 4 =$ _____

   b) $3 \times 3 =$ _____, so $3 \times 6 =$ _____

3. Use each fact to calculate. The first one is partly done for you.

   a) $5 \times 5 = 25$, so $5 \times 6$ is the same as
   _____ 25 + 5 = _____

   b) $2 \times 7 = 14$, so $3 \times 7$ is the same as
   _____

   c) $8 \times 4 = 32$, so $8 \times 3$ is the same as
   _____

### At-Home Help

Here are some strategies to help you multiply. For example, suppose you don't know the product of $4 \times 5$.

**Skip counting up**
You can use a known fact like $2 \times 5 = 10$. Skip count up by adding two groups of 5.
  +5  +5
10, 15, 20

**Skip counting down**
You can use a known fact like $5 \times 5 = 25$. Skip count down by subtracting one group of 5.
$25 - 5 = 20$

**Doubling**
You can double 5 to get $2 \times 5 = 10$, and then double again to get $4 \times 5 = 20$.

4. Calculate.

   a) $2 \times 9 =$ _____   b) $5 \times 7 =$ _____   c) $6 \times 4 =$ _____

5. a) Four students are in Justine's reading group. Each student has three books. How many books do they have in all?

   b) Describe how you calculated the answer.

   _____

# Chapter 6 Lesson 2: Special Products

**GOAL**

Use special strategies to multiply by 8 and 9.

1. Calculate 8 × 9 using each strategy.

   a) doubling
   _____
   _____

   b) first multiplying by 10, and then subtracting
   _____

2. How could you calculate each product? Describe the strategy you would use. Then calculate.

   a) 9 × 5 _____
   _____

   b) 5 × 8 _____
   _____

**At-Home Help**

Here is another strategy to help you multiply.

To multiply by 8 or 9, first multiply by 10, and then subtract.

For example, to calculate 7 × 9, first calculate 7 × 10 = 70. Then subtract 7 to get 70 − 7 = 63.

To calculate 7 × 8, first calculate 7 × 10 = 70. Then subtract two 7s to get 70 − 7 − 7 = 56.

3. Cars have four wheels and many trucks have six wheels.

   a) How many more wheels do eight trucks have than eight cars?

   b) How many more wheels do nine trucks have than nine cars?

44  *Nelson Math Focus 5 Workbook*

# Chapter 6
## Lesson 3 — Relating Multiplication Facts

**GOAL**

Describe how multiplication facts are related.

1. Describe how to use the first multiplication fact to calculate the second fact. The first one is partly done for you.

   a) I know $2 \times 5 = 10$, and I want to know $4 \times 5$.

   I will _double the answer to the first fact._

   $10 + 10 = 20$, so $4 \times 5 =$ _____

   b) I know $3 \times 5 = 15$, and I want to know $6 \times 5$.

   I will _____

   c) I know $10 \times 6 = 60$, and I want to know $9 \times 6$.

   I will _____

   d) I know $7 \times 4 = 28$, and I want to know $7 \times 5$.

   I will _____

---

**At-Home Help**

You can use one multiplication fact to help you calculate another fact.

For example:
I know $4 \times 9 = 36$.

I can use this fact to calculate $5 \times 9$. $5 \times 9$ is the same as $4 \times 9$ plus one more 9. So $5 \times 9 = 36 + 9$, and $5 \times 9 = 45$.

I can use the same fact to calculate $8 \times 9$. 8 is double 4, so $8 \times 9$ is the same as double $4 \times 9$. So $8 \times 9 = 36 + 36$, and $8 \times 9 = 72$.

---

2. Use $4 \times 8 = 32$ to calculate each multiplication fact. Show your work.

   a) $5 \times 8$      b) $8 \times 8$      c) $3 \times 8$

3. Jay knows that $7 \times 7 = 49$.
   How can he use this fact to calculate $7 \times 5$?

Chapter 6: Multiplication

# Chapter 6 Lesson 4: Multiplying by Tens, Hundreds, and Thousands

**GOAL**

Calculate products with multiples of tens, hundreds, or thousands using mental math.

1. Use each fact to calculate.

    a) 5 × 5 tens = 25 tens, so 5 × 50 = _____

    b) 7 × 2 hundreds = 14 hundreds, so 7 × 200 = _____

    c) 4 × 8 tens = 32 tens, so 4 × 80 = _____

    d) 7 × 3 thousands = 21 thousands, so 7 × 3000 = _____

2. Calculate.

    a) 80 × 3 tens = 240 tens, so 80 × 30 = _____

    b) 20 × 9 tens = 180 tens, so 20 × 90 = _____

    c) 10 × 2 hundreds = 20 hundreds, so 10 × 200 = _____

    d) 50 × 3 hundreds = 150 hundreds, so 50 × 300 = _____

**At-Home Help**

When you multiply by tens, hundreds, and thousands, it helps to rename numbers.

For example, calculate 30 × 50.
30 × 50 is the same as
30 × 5 tens.
30 × 5 tens = 150 tens, or 1500.
For example, calculate 4 × 3000.
4 × 3000 is the same as
4 × 3 thousands.
4 × 3 thousands = 12 thousands, or 12 000.

3. Calculate. Explain what you did.

    a) 4 × 200 = _____

    b) 90 × 30 = _____

    c) 6 × 3000 = _____

4. Calculate.

    a) 20 × 30 _____  b) 50 × 60 _____  c) 40 × 70 _____

5. Sydney can make 20 paper cranes in 1 day. How many paper cranes can she expect to make in 20 days?

# Chapter 6 Lesson 5
## Halving and Doubling to Multiply

**GOAL**

Multiply by halving and doubling.

1. Use the half/double strategy to calculate. The first one is done for you.

    a) $8 \times 3 =$ __4 x 6__ , so $8 \times 3 =$ __24__

    b) $20 \times 4 =$ _____ , so $20 \times 4 =$ _____

    c) $6 \times 500 =$ _____ , so $6 \times 500 =$ _____

**At-Home Help**

Here is another strategy to help you multiply.

Divide one number by 2 to get half, and double the other number to make easier numbers to multiply.

For example, to calculate $6 \times 5$, you can use half of 6 and double 5.

$6 \times 5 = 3 \times 10$
$6 \times 5 = 30$

2. Rewrite each equation by making one factor 10, 100, or 1000, and keeping the product the same. The first one is done for you.

    a) $5 \times 4$ is the same as __10 x 2__

    b) $8 \times 500$ is the same as _____

    c) $50 \times 14$ is the same as _____

3. Calculate.

    a) $50 \times 8$    c) $20 \times 500$

    b) $500 \times 18$    d) $12 \times 50$

4. What is the value of 500 toonies?

5. What is the value of 16 $50 bills?

# Chapter 6 Lesson 6
# Multiplying Numbers Close to Tens

**GOAL**

Multiply using a simpler, related question.

1. Calculate the first product. Use the answer to calculate the second product. The first one is partly done for you.

   a) $50 \times 3 = $ __150__ , so $51 \times 3$ is the same as
      __$150 + 3 = $__

   b) $40 \times 6 = $ _____ , so $39 \times 6$ is the same as
      _____

   c) $80 \times 3 = $ _____ , so $82 \times 3$ is the same as
      _____

2. Calculate. Show what you did.

   a) $3 \times 31$ _____
   b) $89 \times 2$ _____
   c) $7 \times 19$ _____
   d) $8 \times 101$ _____

**At-Home Help**

Here is a strategy to help you multiply numbers that are close to tens.

Calculate the easier, related question first. Then add or subtract to answer the original question.

For example, calculate $29 \times 6$.

This question is close to $30 \times 6$. I will calculate this easier question first.

$30 \times 6 = 180$

I need to subtract one 6 to answer the original question.

$180 - 6 = 174$, so $29 \times 6 = 174$

3. A building has 38 windows on each floor.

   a) How many windows are on 2 floors?
   _____

   b) How many windows are on 6 floors?
   _____

4. Rebecca earns $8 every Saturday morning. How much does Rebecca earn in 49 Saturdays?

   _____

*Nelson Math Focus 5 Workbook*

# Chapter 6 Lesson 7: Estimating Products

**GOAL**

Estimate to solve problems.

1. Estimate.

   a) 19 × 5 is about _____

   b) 31 × 2 is about _____

   c) 78 × 3 is about _____

2. 76 students are going on a class trip. The teacher wants to know if 3 buses will be enough to take all the students. 23 students can go on each bus. Why do you think the teacher estimated high by multiplying 25 × 3?

   _____

   _____

3. Estimate. Describe what you did.

   a) 21 × 50

   _____

   b) 89 × 20

   _____

   c) 62 × 39

   _____

4. Owen's class is making kites. Each kite needs 35 m of string. There are 25 students in the class. About how much string does the class need?

   _____

   _____

**At-Home Help**

When you estimate, think about whether to estimate high or to estimate low. For example:

Ami saved 52 $5 bills. She wants to estimate if she has enough money for a $250 bike.

**Solution:** I will estimate low, to make sure there is enough money. I will estimate using 50. 50 × 5 is the same as 25 × 10 = 250. Ami has about $250. She has enough money for the bike.

# Chapter 6 Lesson 8
# Multiplying Two-Digit Numbers

**GOAL**

Multiply two-digit numbers using your choice of strategies.

Jolie and Desmond timed their blinks, breaths, and heartbeats for one minute. They recorded their results in a chart.

|  | Jolie | Desmond |
|---|---|---|
| Blinks in 1 min | 38 | 25 |
| Breaths in 1 min | 15 | 13 |
| Heartbeats in 1 min | 60 | 72 |

1. Use any strategy to calculate. Show your work.

   a) How many times would Jolie's heart beat in 30 min?

   b) How many times would Desmond breathe in 19 min?

   c) How many times would each person blink in 60 min?

2. Write and solve your own question about Jolie or Desmond.

# Multiplying with Base Ten Blocks

**GOAL**

Represent the products of two-digit numbers.

**1.** Complete the multiplication for the model.

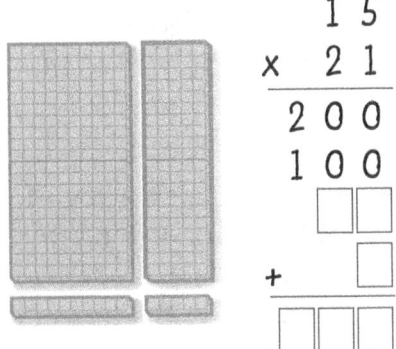

```
      1 5
   ×  2 1
   ─────
    2 0 0
    1 0 0
      ☐ ☐
  +     ☐
   ─────
    ☐ ☐ ☐
```

**At-Home Help**

You can use base ten blocks to model 24 × 13.

Think of 24 as 20 + 4, and 13 as 10 + 3.

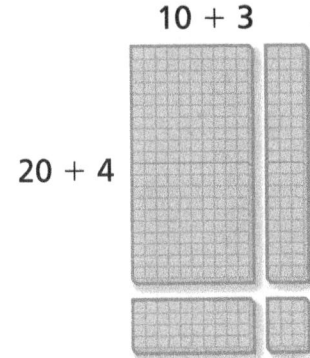

The size of each part of the array is the product of the number of rows and columns.

Add the four products to get the total product.

```
       24
    ×  13
    ─────
      200  (20 × 10)
       60  (20 × 3)
       40  (10 × 4)
    + 12   (4 × 3)
    ─────
      312
```

**2.** Calculate. Sketch a model to help you.

a)   21
   × 21
   ────

b)   17
   × 11
   ────

**3.** Grace has 14 sets of blocks.
Each set has 12 blocks.
How many blocks does she have in total?

Copyright © 2009 by Nelson Education Ltd.    Chapter 6: Multiplication  **51**

# Chapter 6
## Lesson 10 — Multiplying with Arrays

**GOAL**

Multiply two-digit numbers using arrays.

You will need grid paper.

1. **a)** Sketch an array that shows 15 × 12.

   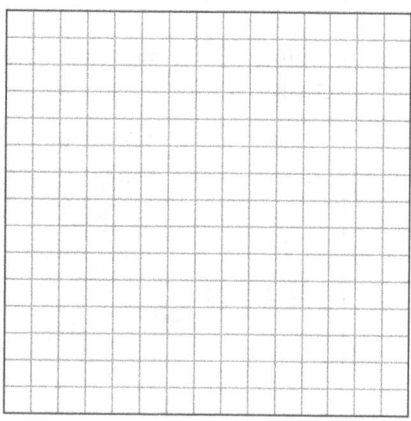

   **b)** Divide your array into four parts that are easier to calculate.

   **c)** Calculate each product and add them to get the total product.

**At-Home Help**

Here is an example of using an array to multiply 18 × 14. This method is very similar to using base ten blocks.

- First, sketch an array of 18 by 14 squares on grid paper.
- Next, divide the array into four parts that are easier to calculate. For example, divide it into 10 × 10, 10 × 8, 4 × 10, and 4 × 8.

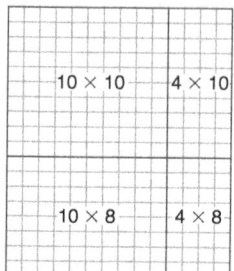

- Add the four products to get the total product: 100 + 80 + 40 + 32 = 252, so 18 × 14 = 252

2. Calculate.

   **a)** 11 × 19     **b)** 23 × 29     **c)** 71 × 42

# Communicating about Multiplication Methods

**GOAL**

Explain your calculation method when solving a problem.

1. Owen explained how he calculated 30 × 81.

   "81 is close to 80, so first I did 30 x 80. Then I added the leftover part to find the total. The answer is 2430."

   Write a better explanation for 30 × 81. Use the Communication Checklist.

   _____

   _____

   _____

   _____

   **At-Home Help**

   **Communication Checklist**
   ✔ Did you explain your thinking?
   ✔ Did you show all the steps?
   ✔ Did you use math language?

2. Ami's house is 72 m away from the school. Over two weeks, Ami walked back and forth 19 times. How many metres did she walk? Show your thinking as completely as possible.

3. There are 30 cards in a set of baseball cards. Sydney has 48 sets of cards in her collection. How many baseball cards does she have?

Copyright © 2009 by Nelson Education Ltd.  Chapter 6: Multiplication  **53**

# Chapter 6    Test Yourself

**Circle the correct answer.**

1. How can you use 4 × 3 = 12 to help you calculate 8 × 3?
   - **A.** multiply 3 by 10 and then subtract 4
   - **B.** skip count from 4 three times
   - **C.** halve the 4 and the 12
   - **D.** double the 4 and the 12

2. Which multiplication fact is the most useful to help you multiply 9 × 5?
   - **A.** 10 × 5 = 50
   - **B.** 8 × 8 = 64
   - **C.** 2 × 3 = 6
   - **D.** 6 × 6 = 36

3. Calculate 30 × 40.
   - **A.** 12
   - **B.** 120
   - **C.** 1200
   - **D.** 12 000

4. Calculate 8 × 3000.
   - **A.** 24
   - **B.** 240
   - **C.** 2400
   - **D.** 24 000

5. Which multiplication fact is the same as 50 × 14?
   - **A.** 51 × 13 = 663
   - **B.** 100 × 7 = 700
   - **C.** 25 × 7 = 175
   - **D.** 100 × 28 = 2800

6. Calculate 40 × 500.
   - **A.** 20 000
   - **B.** 40 000
   - **C.** 10 000
   - **D.** 2000

7. Calculate 4 × 49.
   - **A.** 215
   - **B.** 302
   - **C.** 77
   - **D.** 196

8. Estimate to decide which answer is reasonable for 81 × 19.
   - **A.** 167
   - **B.** 1539
   - **C.** 2970
   - **D.** 735

9. Calculate 33 × 100.
   - **A.** 3300
   - **B.** 330
   - **C.** 33 000
   - **D.** 330 000

10. Calculate 29 × 13.
    - **A.** 389
    - **B.** 358
    - **C.** 377
    - **D.** 319

# Chapter 7 Lesson 1: Recognizing and Creating Equivalent Fractions

**GOAL**

Recognize and create fractions that describe the same amount.

1. Matthew used counters to model a fraction. There are four grey counters in his model. There are eight counters in total.

   **At-Home Help**

   Equivalent fractions are fractions that represent the same part of a whole or the same part of a set.

   $\frac{1}{2}$ is equivalent to $\frac{2}{4}$

   a) Write a fraction that matches Matthew's model. _____

   b) Write an equivalent fraction that matches the model. _____

2. Write two equivalent fractions to describe the grey part of each shape.

   a) 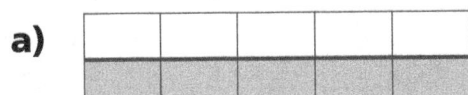    b)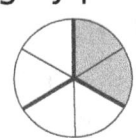

3. Circle the equivalent fractions. Sketch models to help you.

   $\frac{4}{8}$    $\frac{1}{3}$    $\frac{3}{6}$    $\frac{1}{2}$    $\frac{4}{6}$

4. Rebecca modelled a fraction using grey and black stars. Write two equivalent fractions to describe the grey part of Rebecca's model.

Chapter 7: Fractions   55

# Chapter 7 Lesson 2: Using Fractions to Describe Area

**GOAL**

Use different fractions to describe the same part of an area.

Jolie made a puzzle out of squares, rectangles, and triangles.
You can use fractions to describe the different parts of the puzzle.

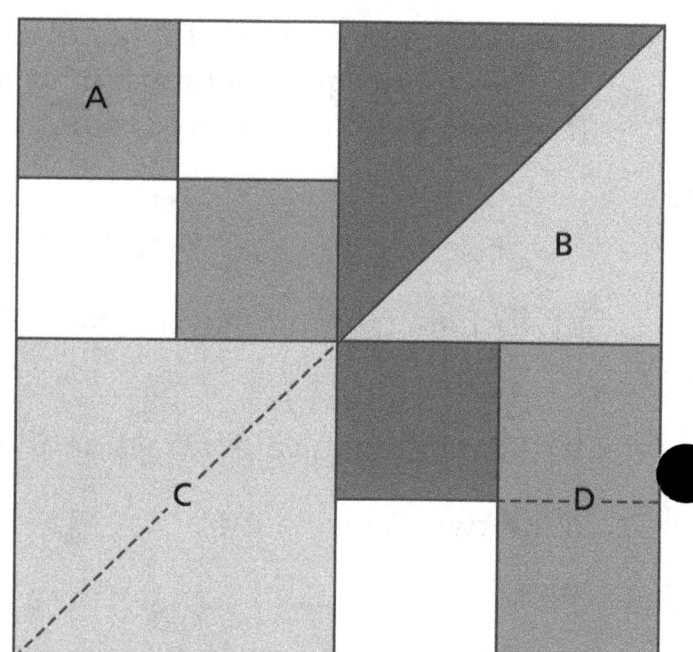

1. a) Look at part A. If the whole puzzle was divided into shapes this size, how many shapes would there be in total? _____

   b) What fraction of the whole puzzle is part A? _____

2. a) Look at part B. If the whole puzzle was divided into shapes this size, how many shapes would there be in total? _____

   b) What fraction of the whole puzzle is part B? _____

3. a) What fraction of the whole puzzle is part C? _____

   b) What fraction of the whole puzzle is part D? _____

4. a) Write an equivalent fraction that describes part C. _____

   b) Write an equivalent fraction that describes part D. _____

5. What fraction of the puzzle is light grey? _____

6. a) What fraction of the puzzle is medium grey? _____

   b) Write an equivalent fraction for the part of the puzzle that is medium grey. _____

56  Nelson Math Focus 5 Workbook

# Chapter 7 Lesson 3: Creating Equivalent Fractions

**GOAL**

Develop a strategy to determine and create equivalent fractions.

1. How do these counters show that $\frac{1}{5}$ is equivalent to $\frac{2}{10}$?

   _____

   _____

   _____

**At-Home Help**

You can model an equivalent fraction problem with counters.

For example: Are $\frac{4}{12}$ and $\frac{1}{3}$ equivalent fractions?

**Solution:** I drew 12 counters. I coloured 4 counters grey. I circled 3 groups. 1 out of the 3 groups is grey. This shows that $\frac{4}{12}$ is equivalent to $\frac{1}{3}$.

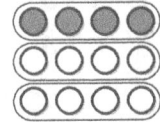

You can also divide or multiply the numerator and denominator of a fraction by the same number to get an equivalent fraction. For example:

$$\frac{4 \div 4}{12 \div 4} = \frac{1}{3}$$

OR

$$\frac{1 \times 4}{3 \times 4} = \frac{4}{12}$$

2. Multiply the numerator and denominator of each fraction to get an equivalent fraction.

   a) $\dfrac{1 \times 2}{4 \times 2} = \underline{\phantom{XX}}$

   b) $\dfrac{2 \times 3}{5 \times 3} = \underline{\phantom{XX}}$

3. Brandon bought three pencil sets. Brandon said that $\frac{1}{3}$ of the pencils were dark grey. Jolie said that $\frac{3}{9}$ of the pencils were dark grey.

   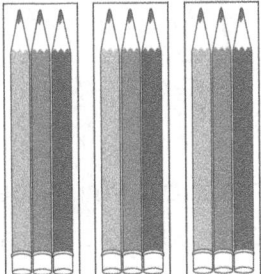

   a) Shade the counters below to show that $\frac{1}{3}$ is equivalent to $\frac{3}{9}$.

   b) Use multiplication or division to show that $\frac{1}{3}$ and $\frac{3}{9}$ are equivalent. Show your work.

# Chapter 7 Lesson 4: Fractions on a Number Line

**GOAL**

Use number lines to compare and order fractions.

You will need tracing paper and scissors.

1. Fill in the blanks with >, <, or =. Use the number line to help you.

   a) $\frac{1}{3}$ ☐ $\frac{2}{3}$   b) $\frac{1}{4}$ ☐ $\frac{1}{3}$   c) $\frac{3}{4}$ ☐ $\frac{2}{3}$

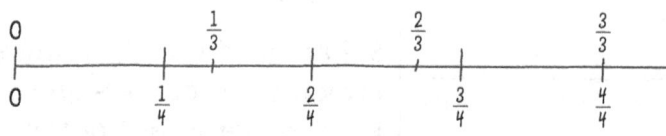

2. Use the number line to help you write these fractions in order from least to greatest.

   $\frac{1}{5}, \frac{3}{4}, \frac{2}{5}, \frac{1}{4}, \frac{4}{4}, \frac{4}{5}$ _____

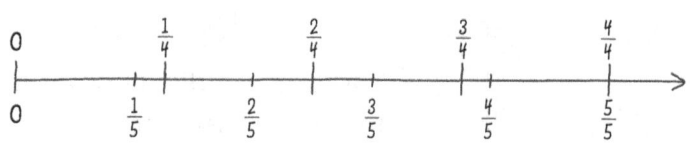

**At-Home Help**

You can use fraction strips to draw a number line. For example, use a $\frac{1}{3}$ fraction strip to mark $\frac{1}{3}, \frac{2}{3}$, and $\frac{3}{3}$ on a number line. Use a $\frac{1}{4}$ fraction strip to mark $\frac{1}{4}, \frac{2}{4}, \frac{3}{4}$, and $\frac{4}{4}$ on the same number line.

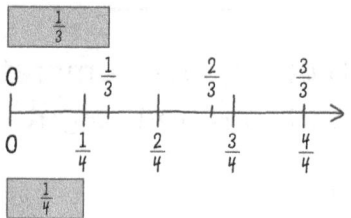

Now you have a number line that you can use to compare fractions in thirds with fractions in fourths.

3. a) Trace and cut out the fraction strips below. Use your fraction strips to complete the number line.

   b) Use your number line to order these fractions from least to greatest.

   $\frac{4}{5}, \frac{2}{5}, \frac{2}{3}, \frac{1}{5}, \frac{3}{3}, \frac{1}{3}$ _____

# Chapter 7 Lesson 5: Comparing Fractions

**GOAL**

Compare two fractions using equivalent fractions.

1. Compare each pair of fractions using < or >.

   a) $\frac{3}{8} \square \frac{3}{4}$   b) $\frac{2}{3} \square \frac{2}{6}$   c) $\frac{2}{2} \square \frac{5}{7}$

2. Write an equivalent fraction for the first fraction. Compare it with the second fraction.

   a) $\frac{1}{3}$ and $\frac{1}{6}$

   b) $\frac{2}{3}$ and $\frac{5}{9}$

3. Compare each pair of fractions using < or >. Use the diagrams to help you.

   a) $\frac{3}{5} \square \frac{4}{10}$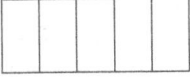

   b) $\frac{2}{3} \square \frac{3}{4}$

4. Compare each pair of fractions using < or >.

   a) $\frac{1}{5} \square \frac{3}{10}$   b) $\frac{5}{7} \square \frac{5}{14}$   c) $\frac{1}{5} \square \frac{1}{3}$   d) $\frac{4}{6} \square \frac{5}{12}$

**At-Home Help**

You can use equivalent fractions to compare two fractions with different denominators.

For example: Which is greater, $\frac{3}{4}$ or $\frac{4}{6}$?

**Solution:** Determine equivalent fractions that are easier to compare. For example, multiply the top and bottom of the first fraction by 3 to get an equivalent fraction in twelfths.

$$\frac{3 \times 3}{4 \times 3} = \frac{9}{12}$$

Multiply the top and bottom of the second fraction by 2 to get an equivalent fraction in twelfths.

$$\frac{4 \times 2}{6 \times 2} = \frac{8}{12}$$

Now compare the two fractions. $\frac{9}{12}$ is greater than $\frac{8}{12}$, so $\frac{3}{4}$ is greater than $\frac{4}{6}$.

# Chapter 7 Lesson 6: Using Decimals and Fractions

**GOAL**

Represent and write amounts as equivalent decimals and equivalent fractions.

1. Each square on the thousandths grid represents 0.001, or $\frac{1}{1000}$, or one thousandth.

   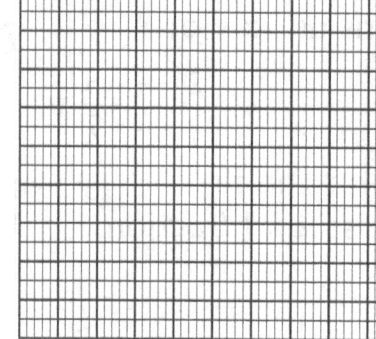

   **At-Home Help**

   You can compare decimal thousandths with fractions that have a denominator of 1000.

   For example:

   0.003 is the same as $\frac{3}{1000}$.

   0.025 is the same as $\frac{25}{1000}$.

   0.700 is the same as $\frac{700}{1000}$.

   a) Shade $\frac{300}{1000}$ on the grid.

   b) What is the decimal form of $\frac{300}{1000}$? _____

   c) What is an equivalent fraction for $\frac{300}{1000}$? _____

2. Write a decimal thousandth for each fraction. Use the thousandth grid to help you.

   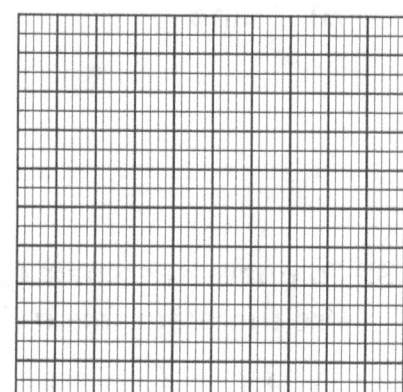

   a) $\frac{600}{1000}$ _____   c) $\frac{5}{1000}$ _____

   b) $\frac{80}{1000}$ _____   d) $\frac{720}{1000}$ _____

3. Write a fraction in thousandths for each decimal.

   a) 0.050 _____   c) 0.192 _____

   b) 0.009 _____   d) 0.700 _____

4. Write a fraction in hundredths for each decimal.

   a) 0.040 _____   c) 0.700 _____

   b) 0.120 _____   d) 0.540 _____

# Using Equivalent Decimals

**Chapter 7 Lesson 7**

**GOAL**

Compare and order fractions and decimals using equivalents.

1. Compare $\frac{9}{1000}$ and 0.09.

    a) Rename $\frac{9}{1000}$ as a decimal. _____
    Compare the two numbers.
    Which number is less? _____

    b) Rename 0.09 as a fraction in thousandths.
    _____
    Compare the two numbers.
    Which number is less? _____

2. Compare each pair of numbers using <, >, or =.

    a) $\frac{1}{1000}$ ☐ 0.001

    b) $\frac{4}{100}$ ☐ 0.05

    c) 0.033 ☐ $\frac{5}{1000}$

    d) 0.1 ☐ $\frac{9}{100}$

3. Sydney has 7 dimes, or 0.70 of a dollar.
   Owen has 42 pennies, or $\frac{42}{100}$ of a dollar.
   Who has more money? Explain.

   _____
   _____

4. There are 1000 students at Lakeview School.
   0.40 of the students have a pet cat.
   70 of the students have a pet hamster.
   Do more students have cats or hamsters? Show your work.

   _____
   _____

**At-Home Help**

To compare a fraction with a decimal, you can rename the fraction as a decimal. Or, you can rename the decimal as a fraction.

For example:
Which is greater, $\frac{8}{10}$ or 0.055?

**Solution 1:** $\frac{8}{10}$ means eight tenths, or 0.8.
0.8 is greater than 0.055.

**Solution 2:** 0.055 means 55 thousandths, or $\frac{55}{1000}$.
$\frac{8}{10}$ is equivalent to $\frac{800}{1000}$.
$\frac{800}{1000}$ is greater than $\frac{55}{1000}$.

# Chapter 7 Lesson 8: Solving Problems Using Logical Reasoning

## GOAL
Use logical reasoning to solve fraction and decimal problems.

1. Three students wrote fraction riddles.

   **Matthew's Riddle**
   Clue 1: My fraction is greater than $\frac{1}{2}$.
   Clue 2: The denominator is 100.
   Clue 3: The numerator has two digits: 3 and 7.

   **At-Home Help**
   Follow these steps to solve problems:
   - Understand the problem.
   - Make a plan to solve the problem.
   - Carry out the plan.
   - Look back to make sure your solution makes sense.

   a) What is Matthew's fraction?
   _____
   _____

   **Rachel's Riddle**
   Clue 1: The fraction is equivalent to $\frac{1}{3}$.
   Clue 2: The sum of the numerator and denominator is 16.

   **René's Riddle**
   Clue 1: The fraction is equivalent to $\frac{4}{5}$.
   Clue 2: The numerator and denominator can both be divided by 3.
   Clue 3: The denominator is an odd number.

   b) What is Rachel's fraction?
   _____
   _____
   _____
   _____

   c) What is René's fraction?
   _____
   _____
   _____
   _____

62  Nelson Math Focus 5 Workbook

# Chapter 7   Test Yourself

**Circle the correct answer.**

1. Which fraction is equivalent to $\frac{2}{3}$?

   A. $\frac{1}{3}$    B. $\frac{4}{6}$    C. $\frac{3}{4}$    D. $\frac{2}{6}$

2. Which equivalent fractions describe the grey part of the picture?

   A. $\frac{1}{4}$ and $\frac{2}{8}$    B. $\frac{3}{4}$ and $\frac{6}{8}$    C. $\frac{8}{8}$ and $\frac{2}{2}$    D. $\frac{4}{8}$ and $\frac{1}{2}$

3. $\frac{8}{10}$ of the counters below are shaded. What other fraction can you use to describe the shaded counters?

   A. $\frac{4}{5}$    B. $\frac{1}{2}$    C. $\frac{3}{4}$    D. $\frac{1}{8}$

4. Use the number line to order these fractions from least to greatest: $\frac{4}{5}, \frac{1}{4}, \frac{1}{5}, \frac{2}{4}$.

   A. $\frac{1}{4}, \frac{1}{5}, \frac{2}{4}, \frac{4}{5}$    B. $\frac{1}{5}, \frac{1}{4}, \frac{2}{4}, \frac{4}{5}$    C. $\frac{1}{4}, \frac{1}{5}, \frac{4}{5}, \frac{2}{4}$    D. $\frac{4}{5}, \frac{2}{4}, \frac{1}{5}, \frac{1}{4}$

5. Which comparison is correct?

   A. $\frac{1}{3} < \frac{1}{6}$    B. $\frac{1}{2} > \frac{4}{5}$    C. $\frac{1}{5} < \frac{3}{10}$    D. $\frac{9}{10} < \frac{4}{10}$

6. What is the decimal name for $\frac{55}{1000}$?

   A. 0.55    B. 0.055    C. 5.5    D. 0.0055

7. Which comparison is correct?

   A. $\frac{1}{100} < 0.1$    B. $\frac{20}{1000} > \frac{5}{100}$    C. $0.04 < \frac{1}{100}$    D. $\frac{9}{10} < 0.09$

8. Ami wrote a fraction riddle: "My denominator is 100. My fraction is equivalent to 0.700." What is Ami's fraction?

   A. $\frac{700}{1000}$    B. $\frac{7}{100}$    C. $\frac{7}{10}$    D. $\frac{70}{100}$

# Chapter 8 Lesson 1: Measuring Length in Millimetres

**GOAL**

Measure length using millimetres.

You will need a ruler.

**At-Home Help**

A **millimetre (mm)** is a unit of length that is about the thickness of a dime. There are 10 millimetres in 1 centimetre.

For example, the line below is 14 mm long. You can also say that it is close to 1.5 cm long.

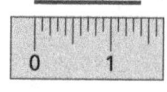

1. Draw a line to represent each length.

   a) 20 mm

   b) 2 cm

   c) 37 mm

   d) 52 mm

2. How many centimetres are in each length?

   a) 10 mm = _____ cm

   b) 30 mm = _____ cm

   c) 100 mm = _____ cm        e) 720 mm = _____ cm

   d) 150 mm = _____ cm        f) 380 mm = _____ cm

3. Tai used a 30 cm ruler to measure a book. The book was 440 mm long.

   a) Is the book longer or shorter than Tai's ruler? _____

   b) How many centimetres long is the book? _____ cm

4. Rachel measured an object. It was 180 mm long.

   a) How many centimetres long is the object? _____ cm

   b) What object could be 180 mm long? _____

5. Owen measured an object. It was 490 mm long.

   a) How many centimetres long is the object? _____ cm

   b) There are 100 cm in a metre. Owen says his object is close to 0.5 m. Is he correct? Explain why or why not. _____

# Chapter 8 Lesson 2: Estimating Length

**GOAL**

Use referents to estimate length in millimetres, centimetres, and metres.

1. Would you use millimetres, centimetres, or metres to measure each object?

    a) a pencil _____

    b) an ant _____

    c) a house _____

    d) a piece of bread _____

2. Use the width of your finger to estimate the length of each object in centimetres.

    a) your pen or pencil _____

    b) your nose _____

    c) this workbook _____

### At-Home Help

You can use parts of your body to help you estimate length. For example:

- Your fingernail is about 1 mm thick.
- Your finger is about 1 cm wide.
- The palm of your hand is about 5 cm wide.
- Your arm is about 0.5 m long.

Use a ruler to check these measurements on yourself.

3. Use the thickness of your fingernail to estimate the length of each line in millimetres.

    a) —   about _____ mm    b) ——   about _____ mm

4. Estimate the width of each object. Use any unit of measurement.

    a) your mouth _____

    b) a shoelace _____

    c) your knee _____

    d) your bed _____

5. Owen says that he is 150 mm tall. Jolie thinks that sounds too short. Is 150 mm too short for a person's height? Explain your thinking.

_____

# Chapter 8 Lesson 3: Exploring Perimeter

**GOAL**

Design and construct different rectangles with a given perimeter.

1. Rachel used a ribbon that is 36 cm long to frame a rectangular drawing. What size could her drawing be? Fill in the blanks to identify all the rectangles with whole-centimetre sides that have a perimeter of 36 cm.

**At-Home Help**

Perimeter is the distance around a shape. For example, the perimeter of this rectangle is 5 cm + 10 cm + 5 cm + 10 cm = 30 cm.

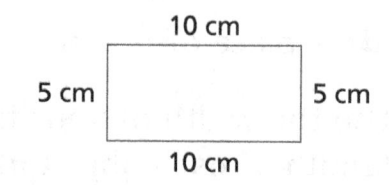

3 + __15__ + 3 + __15__ = 36, so the sides are 3 cm and _____ cm

4 + _____ + 4 + _____ = 36, so the sides are 4 cm and _____ cm

5 + _____ + 5 + _____ = 36, so the sides are 5 cm and _____ cm

6 + _____ + 6 + _____ = 36, so the sides are 6 cm and _____ cm

7 + _____ + 7 + _____ = 36, so the sides are 7 cm and _____ cm

8 + _____ + 8 + _____ = 36, so the sides are 8 cm and _____ cm

2. A rectangular garden has a perimeter of 60 m.

   a) List four different rectangles with whole-metre sides that have a perimeter of 60 m.

   b) One of the sides of the garden is 10 m long. What are the lengths of the other sides?

# Perimeters and Areas of Rectangles

Chapter 8 Lesson 4

**GOAL**

Compare rectangles with the same perimeter or the same area.

1. Determine the area and the perimeter of each rectangle.

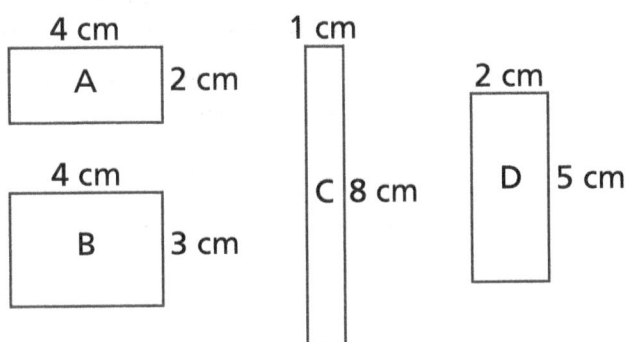

A: perimeter: _____ cm, area: _____ cm²

B: perimeter: _____ cm, area: _____ cm²

C: perimeter: _____ cm, area: _____ cm²

D: perimeter: _____ cm, area: _____ cm²

**At-Home Help**

Area is the number of square units needed to cover a surface.

A **square centimetre (cm²)** is a unit of measurement for area. The shaded diagram shows 1 cm², or one square centimetre. The rectangle below it has an area of 2 cm².

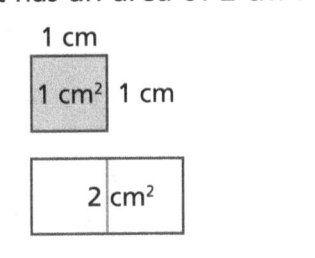

2. a) Sketch a 6 cm by 4 cm rectangle on the grid. Label it Shape 1.

   b) Sketch a different rectangle with the same perimeter as Shape 1.

   c) Sketch another rectangle with the same area as Shape 1.

Copyright © 2009 by Nelson Education Ltd.      Chapter 8: Measurement    **67**

# Chapter 8 Lesson 5: Measuring and Comparing Volumes

**GOAL**

Determine and compare the volumes of 3-D objects, and create 3-D objects with the same volume.

**You will need 24 cubes.**

**At-Home Help**

Volume is the amount of space occupied by a 3-D object. For example, this structure has a volume of 3 cubes.

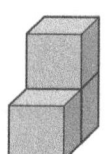

1. What is the volume of each structure?

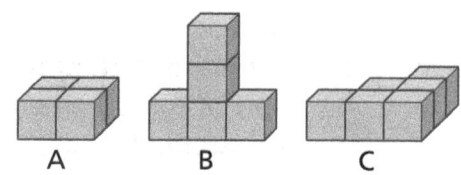

A     B     C

A: _____ cubes

B: _____ cubes

C: _____ cubes

2. a) Use 12 cubes to build a box with a rectangular base. This structure is called a rectangular prism.

   How many layers are in your prism? _____ layers

   How many cubes are in each layer of your prism? _____ cubes

   b) Now build a different rectangular prism using the same 12 cubes.

   How many layers are in your prism? _____ layers

   How many cubes are in each layer of your prism? _____ cubes

3. a) Build a rectangular prism with a volume of 24 cubes.

   How many layers are in your prism? _____ layers

   How many cubes are in each layer of your prism? _____ cubes

   b) Now build a different rectangular prism with a volume of 24 cubes.

   How many layers are in your prism? _____ layers

   How many cubes are in each layer of your prism? _____ cubes

68 Nelson Math Focus 5 Workbook

# Chapter 8 Lesson 6: Measuring Volume in Cubic Centimetres

**GOAL**

Estimate, measure, and compare volumes using cubic centimetres.

You will need 24 cubes.

1. Each rectangular prism below was built using centimetre cubes.

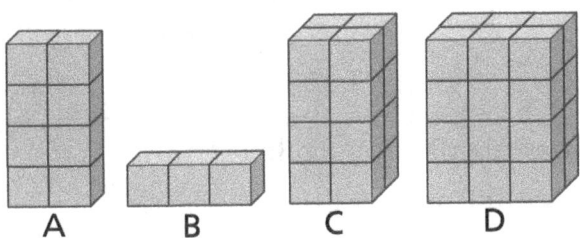

**At-Home Help**

A **cubic centimetre ($cm^3$)** is the volume of a cube that is 1 cm long, 1 cm wide, and 1 cm high.

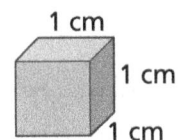

Model each prism using cubes. What is the volume of each prism in cubic centimetres?

A: _____ $cm^3$

B: _____ $cm^3$

C: _____ $cm^3$

D: _____ $cm^3$

2. Owen built a rectangular prism with a volume of 20 $cm^3$. His rectangle was long and thin. Sydney built a rectangular prism with the same volume. Her rectangle had a square base.

   a) Use cubes to model Owen's and Sydney's rectangular prisms.

   b) Sketch your models. Label the length, width, and height in centimetres.

# Chapter 8 Lesson 7: Measuring Volume in Cubic Metres

**GOAL**

Estimate, measure, and compare volumes using cubic metres.

You will need a metre stick.

**At-Home Help**

A **cubic metre ($m^3$)** is a cube that is 1 m long, 1 m high, and 1 m wide. For example, the volume of a refrigerator might be about 1 $m^3$.

1. **a)** Use a metre stick to measure the width, length, and height of a dresser.

    width: _____ m     length: _____ m

    height: _____ m

   **b)** Do you think the volume of a dresser is greater than, less than, or about the same as a cubic metre? Explain.

   _____

   _____

2. **a)** List three objects in your house that have a volume less than 1 $m^3$.

   _____

   **b)** List three objects in your house that have a volume greater than 1 $m^3$.

   _____

3. Go to your kitchen. Assume that the refrigerator has a volume of 1 $m^3$. (It may actually be a little smaller or larger.)

   **a)** About how many refrigerators could you fit in the kitchen, if you stacked them on top of each other? _____

   **b)** Estimate the volume of your kitchen. _____

4. Which objects might be measured using cubic metres? Circle the pictures.

# Chapter 8 Lesson 8
# Exploring Litres and Millilitres

**GOAL**

Measure and compare capacities.

You will need water, 125 mL and 250 mL measuring cups, and several empty containers.

1. **a)** Label four empty containers 1 to 4.

   **b)** Fill a container with water. Then pour the water carefully out into a measuring cup. Record the number of times you can fill the measuring cup. Use this information to estimate the capacity of the container.

   **c)** Repeat part b) for the other three containers.

   **d)** Record your procedure and your results.

   Container 1:

   Container 2:

   Container 3:

   Container 4:

**At-Home Help**

**Capacity** is the amount that a container can hold.

A **millilitre (mL)** is a unit of capacity. For example, 1 mL describes the amount of water that a hollow centimetre cube could hold.

A **litre (L)** is a larger unit of capacity. 1 L = 1000 mL. For example, milk is often sold in 1 L containers.

# Chapter 8 Lesson 9: Estimating and Measuring Capacity

**GOAL**

Estimate, measure, and compare capacities using litres and millilitres.

You will need water, some measuring spoons and cups (e.g., 5 mL, 50 mL, 125 mL, 250 mL), and several empty containers. Choose different containers than in Lesson 8.

**At-Home Help**

Here are some capacities:
- a small spoon: about 5 mL
- a can of juice: about 350 mL
- a large milk carton: about 2 L
- a bathroom sink: about 10 L

1. Circle the measuring cup you would use to estimate the capacity of each container.

   a) an aquarium
   
   1 L cup
   250 mL cup
   50 mL cup

   b) a drinking glass
   
   1 L cup
   250 mL cup
   50 mL cup

   c) a serving spoon
   
   1 L cup
   250 mL cup
   50 mL cup

2. Choose an empty container that you think has a capacity greater than 500 mL.

   a) Estimate the capacity of the container. _____
   
   b) Measure the capacity of the container. _____

3. Choose an empty container that you think has a capacity less than 125 mL.

   a) Estimate the capacity of the container. _____
   
   b) Measure the capacity of the container. _____

4. Choose an empty container that you think has a capacity greater than 1 L.

   a) Estimate the capacity of the container. _____
   
   b) Measure the capacity of the container. _____

5. Write the equal measurements in millilitres or litres.

   a) 1 L = _____ mL      b) 3000 mL = _____ L      c) 6.5 L = _____ mL

6. Order these capacities from greatest to least: 50 mL, 2000 mL, 5 L, 1 L, 250 mL.

   _____

# Chapter 8 Lesson 10: Solving Problems Using a Chart

**GOAL**

Solve problems using a chart to list combinations.

1. Brandon has three scoops for measuring. He can use one scoop, two scoops, or all three full scoops at the same time.

   Fill in the last column of the chart to show all the different amounts Brandon can measure at one time.

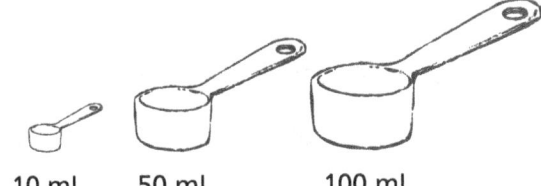

10 mL     50 mL     100 mL

**Ways Brandon Can Measure**

|                 | 10 mL | 50 mL | 100 mL | Total  |
|-----------------|-------|-------|--------|--------|
| Using 1 scoop   | ✓     |       |        | 10 mL  |
|                 |       | ✓     |        |        |
|                 |       |       | ✓      |        |
| Using 2 scoops  | ✓     | ✓     |        |        |
|                 |       | ✓     | ✓      |        |
|                 | ✓     |       | ✓      |        |
| Using 3 scoops  | ✓     | ✓     | ✓      |        |

2. Ami has three measuring cups. What possible amounts can she measure at one time if she uses one cup, two cups, or all three full cups? Fill in the chart to show your work.

100 mL     250 mL     500 mL

**Title:** _____

|   |   |   |   |
|---|---|---|---|
|   |   |   |   |
|   |   |   |   |
|   |   |   |   |
|   |   |   |   |
|   |   |   |   |
|   |   |   |   |
|   |   |   |   |

# Chapter 8    Test Yourself

**Circle the correct answer.**

1. Sydney measured an object. It was 5 mm wide. Which object did Sydney measure?

   A. her math textbook    C. her shoe
   B. her baby fingernail   D. her shirt

2. Jay measured an object. It was 30 cm long. Which object did Jay measure?

   A. his notebook    B. his bicycle    C. his finger    D. his house

3. What is the perimeter of this rectangle?

   A. 14 cm    B. 20 cm    C. 28 cm    D. 34 cm

4. What is the area of this rectangle?

   A. 48 cm²    B. 22 cm²    C. 100 cm²    D. 72 cm²

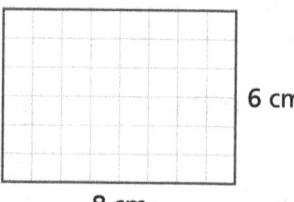
6 cm
8 cm

5. This structure looks the same on both sides. What is its volume?

   A. 2 cubes    B. 3 cubes    C. 4 cubes    D. 5 cubes

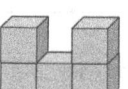

6. A box has a volume of 100 cm³. Which object is the box most likely to hold?

   A. a pencil    B. a TV    C. shoes    D. a refrigerator

7. Which object is most likely to have a volume of about 100 m³?

   A. a book    B. a room    C. a person    D. a building

8. How much juice are you likely to drink at lunch?

   A. 10 L    B. 2 L    C. 250 mL    D. 15 mL

9. Tai has three measuring scoops: 5 mL, 50 mL, and 250 mL. What possible amounts can he measure at one time if he uses any two full scoops?

   A. 305 mL or 505 mL           C. 55 mL, 255 mL, or 300 mL
   B. 5 mL, 50 mL, or 250 mL     D. 100 mL, 200 mL, or 300 mL

# Chapter 9 Lesson 1: Division Fact Strategies

**GOAL**

Use strategies to relate unknown facts to known facts.

1. Use the array to complete each equation.

   a) 15 ÷ 5 = _____

   b) 25 ÷ 5 = _____

**At-Home Help**

You can use arrays to complete division equations. For example: 18 ÷ 3 =

I will use 18 counters to make an array with 3 rows.

There are 6 counters in each row, so 18 ÷ 3 = 6.

2. Sketch an array to determine each quotient.

   a) 12 ÷ 3 = _____

   b) 24 ÷ 4 = _____

   c) 21 ÷ 3 = _____

   d) 40 ÷ 5 = _____

   e) 42 ÷ 6 = _____

# Chapter 9 Lesson 2: Dividing by Halving

**GOAL**

Relate division facts by halving.

1. 20 people are sitting in 4 equal groups. How many people are in each group? Use dividing by 2 to calculate the number of people in each group.

**At-Home Help**

You can divide by halving.

For example:
16 people are sitting in 4 equal groups. How many people are in each group?

**Solution:** I can divide 16 by 2 to make 2 groups of 8.
I can divide these 2 groups by 2 to make 4 groups of 4.
There are 4 people in each group.

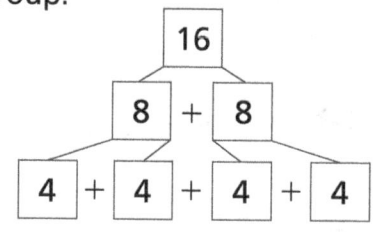

2. Jolie brought 72 cookies to class. She has 8 bags of cookies with the same number in each bag. How many cookies are in each bag?

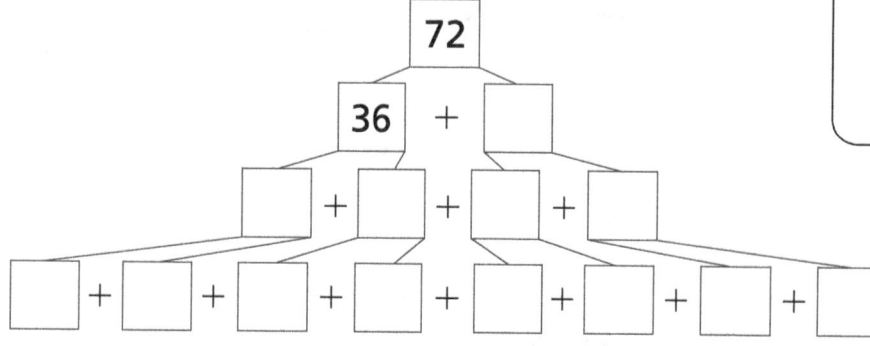

3. Calculate each quotient by dividing by 2 as many times as necessary. Show your work.

   a) $24 \div 4 =$ _____   b) $64 \div 8 =$ _____   c) $40 \div 4 =$ _____

76 *Nelson Math Focus 5 Workbook*

# Chapter 9 Lesson 3: Dividing Tens and Hundreds

**GOAL**

Divide tens and hundreds by one-digit numbers.

1. Rename, and then calculate. Show your work.

   a) 400 ÷ 2 = _____

   b) 600 ÷ 2 = _____

   c) 120 ÷ 6 = _____

**At-Home Help**

You can rename numbers to help you divide.

**Example 1:** Calculate 800 ÷ 4 by renaming 800 as 8 hundreds.
8 hundreds ÷ 4 = 2 hundreds
So 800 ÷ 4 = 200.

**Example 2:** Calculate 120 ÷ 3 by renaming 120 as 12 tens.
12 tens ÷ 3 = 4 tens
So 120 ÷ 3 = 40.

2. Calculate.

   a) 240 ÷ 4 = _____
   b) 360 ÷ 9 = _____
   c) 150 ÷ 3 = _____
   d) 480 ÷ 8 = _____
   e) _____ = 900 ÷ 3
   f) _____ = 270 ÷ 9

3. Tai sketched base ten blocks to calculate 140 ÷ 7. Explain how Tai can calculate the quotient.

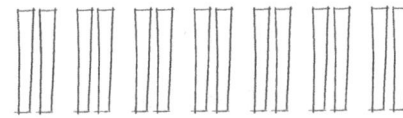

_____

_____

4. Sketch base ten blocks to show how calculating 800 ÷ 4 is like calculating 8 ÷ 4. Explain your sketch.

# Chapter 9 Lesson 4: Estimating Quotients

**GOAL**

Use personal strategies to estimate quotients.

1. At Lakeport Zoo, 119 animals are in 4 groups that are mostly equal. About how many animals are in each group?

**At-Home Help**

You can estimate a quotient by choosing a nearby number that is easier to divide.

For example: Estimate 144 ÷ 3.
144 is close to 150.
150 ÷ 3 is the same as
15 tens ÷ 3 = 5 tens, or 50.
The answer is close to 50.

2. Estimate each quotient by filling in the blanks.

   a) 163 ÷ 2

   163 is close to __16__ tens.

   __16__ tens ÷ 2 = __8__ tens

   So 163 ÷ 2 is about _____.

   b) 237 ÷ 8

   237 is close to _____ tens.

   _____ tens ÷ 8 = _____ tens

   So 237 ÷ 8 is about _____.

   c) 418 ÷ 6

   418 is close to _____ tens.

   _____ tens ÷ 6 = _____ tens

   So 418 ÷ 6 is about _____.

   d) 631 ÷ 9

   631 is close to _____ tens.

   _____ tens ÷ 9 = _____ tens

   So 631 ÷ 9 is about _____.

3. Estimate each quotient.

   a) 98 ÷ 5 _____

   b) 324 ÷ 8 _____

4. Owen bought 6 art posters for $311. About how much did each poster cost?

# Exploring Division with Greater Numbers

**GOAL**

Use personal strategies to solve division problems.

**At-Home Help**

Here are some strategies for solving division problems:
- Sketch an array.
- Divide by halving.
- Rename as tens or hundreds.
- Estimate by choosing a nearby number that is easier to divide.

1. Jolie has 808 g of modelling clay. She wants to make 4 creatures that have the same mass. To calculate each mass, Jolie uses base ten blocks to model 808 g.

   Divide Jolie's base ten blocks into 4 equal groups to represent 4 creatures.
   Sketch your groups.
   What is the mass of each creature?

2. Tai divided 204 g of modelling clay into 4 equal parts. What is the mass of each part? (Hint: Sketch 20 tens and 4 ones blocks.)

3. Use any strategy to solve each division problem.
   a) 366 g of modelling clay, divided into 6 equal parts: 366 ÷ 6 = _____
   b) 464 g of modelling clay, divided into 8 equal parts: 464 ÷ 8 = _____

# Chapter 9
## Lesson 6: Using Subtraction to Divide

**GOAL**

Divide by subtracting repeatedly.

1. Sydney calculated 210 ÷ 6 using a number line. She started at 210 and subtracted sixes.

   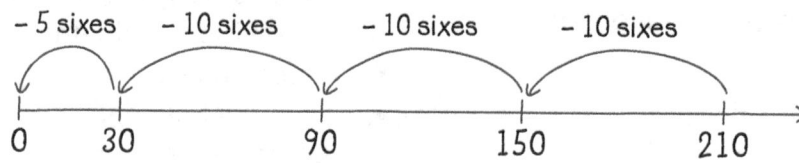

   Use Sydney's number line to calculate the quotient. Show your work.

**At-Home Help**

You can divide by subtracting.
For example:
Calculate 154 ÷ 7.
I will subtract sevens from 154.
I will start by subtracting 10 sevens, or 70. 154 − 70 = 84
I will subtract 10 more sevens.
84 − 70 = 14

I know there are 2 sevens in 14. I will add all the sevens together. 10 + 10 + 2 = 22, so 157 ÷ 7 = 22.

2. Calculate 115 ÷ 5 by subtracting equal groups. Use the number line. 115 ÷ 5 = _____

   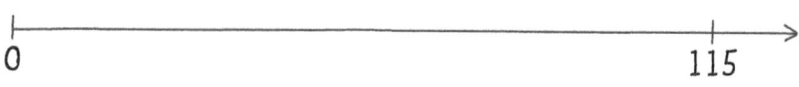

3. 175 students were placed in equal groups for a game.

    a) If the students were put in groups of 5, how many groups were there?

    b) If the students were put in groups of 7, how many groups were there?

# Chapter 9 Lesson 7: Dividing by Sharing

**GOAL**

Divide three-digit numbers by one-digit numbers using models and symbols.

1. Matthew made a plan to calculate 176 ÷ 8.

   Step 1: I need to share 176 base ten blocks into 8 groups.

   I will model 176 as 17 tens and 6 ones.

   Step 2: I can't share 17 tens or 6 ones into 8 groups.

   So I will regroup 176 as 16 tens and 16 ones.

   Step 3: I will share 16 tens and 16 ones into 8 groups.

   Use Matthew's plan to calculate. Sketch your groupings of base ten blocks.

   **At-Home Help**

   You can divide by sharing. For example: Calculate 316 ÷ 3.
   I will model 316 using base ten blocks.

   I can share the 3 hundreds among 3 groups. I will rename the 10 and 6 ones as 16 ones. Now I can share the 16 ones among 3 groups, too.

   Each group has 1 hundred and 5 ones, and there is 1 left over. So 316 ÷ 3 = 105, with 1 left over.

2. Calculate.

   a) 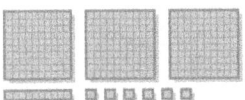  b) 9)198  c) 5)507

   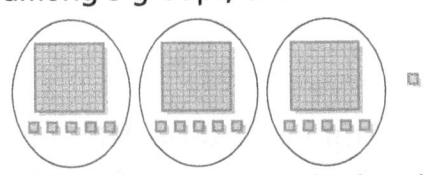

3. Desmond sorted his 187 baseball cards into groups of 6. How many groups did Desmond make? Show your work.

# Chapter 9 Lesson 8: Describing Remainders as Decimals

**GOAL**

Solve division problems with decimal remainders.

You can use quarters and dimes to help you.

1. Express each remainder as a decimal. Use quarters.

   a) $183 ÷ 6 = $30 R3

   b) $146 ÷ 8 = $18 R2

**At-Home Help**

You can use coins to express a remainder as a decimal. For example, $172 ÷ 8 = $21 R4. Express the remainder as a decimal.

**Solution:** $4 is the same as 16 quarters. I will share 16 quarters into 8 groups. There are 2 quarters, or $0.50, in each group.
So $172 ÷ 8 = $21.50.

2. Ami is dividing $82 among her 10 friends. She calculates that each friend will get $8, with $2 left over. Finish Ami's calculation. How much money does each friend get? Use dimes.

3. Five people bought lunch together for $27. Everyone ordered the same thing. How much should each person pay?

82  Nelson Math Focus 5 Workbook                    Copyright © 2009 by Nelson Education Ltd.

# Interpreting Remainders

**GOAL**

Decide how to deal with the remainder in a division problem.

1. It takes 6 pieces of wood to make a box. Rachel's class has 302 pieces of wood.

   a) How many boxes can the class make?

   b) What did you do with the remainder? Why?
   _____
   _____

   **At-Home Help**

   Read the problem to decide what to do with the remainder. For example, sometimes you can ignore the remainder. Sometimes you can use the nearest whole number. Sometimes you can express the remainder as a decimal.

2. Mateo is buying pencils for the school fair. There are 5 pencils in each package. Mateo needs 68 pencils.

   a) How many packages should he buy?

   b) What did you do with the remainder? Why?
   _____
   _____

3. Six students earned $243. They divided the money equally.

   a) How much money did each student get?

   b) What did you do with the remainder? Why?
   _____

# Chapter 9 Lesson 10: Solving Problems by Guessing and Testing

**GOAL**

Guess and test to solve division problems.

1. 240 cans were packed in equal boxes. There were fewer than 10 boxes. How many boxes could there be? List 3 possibilities.

**At-Home Help**

You can use guessing and testing to solve division problems. First, guess what you think the answer might be. Then check your answer. If necessary, guess again, using a higher or lower number.

2. Some friends sold 125 magazines to raise money for a trip. There were fewer than 10 people in the group. Each person sold the same number of magazines.

   a) How many people were in the group? Use guessing and testing to solve.

   b) How many magazines did each person in the group sell?

3. Another group sold 336 magazines. There were fewer than 10 people in the group. Each person sold the same number of magazines.

   a) How many people could be in the group? List 3 possibilities.

   b) For each possibility, how many magazines did each person sell?

84 *Nelson Math Focus 5 Workbook* — Copyright © 2009 by Nelson Education Ltd.

# Chapter 9    Test Yourself

**Circle the correct answer.**

1. Calculate 35 ÷ 7.
   A. 1       B. 3       C. 5       D. 7

2. Calculate 42 ÷ 6.
   A. 6       B. 5       C. 8       D. 7

3. Calculate 120 ÷ 6.
   A. 10      B. 20      C. 50      D. 30

4. Calculate 400 ÷ 2.
   A. 200     B. 150     C. 75      D. 80

5. Calculate 540 ÷ 9.
   A. 50      B. 30      C. 14      D. 60

6. Estimate 322 ÷ 8. Use your estimate to identify the correct answer below.
   A. 20.25   B. 50.25   C. 30.25   D. 40.25

7. Calculate 76 ÷ 4.
   A. 17      B. 19      C. 21      D. 23

8. Jay and 5 friends baked 414 muffins for a bake sale. Each person baked the same number of muffins. How many muffins did each person bake?
   A. 69 muffins    B. 82 muffins    C. 23 muffins    D. 77 muffins

9. Cara divided 123 marbles equally into 6 bags. How many marbles were left over?
   A. 1 marble      B. 2 marbles     C. 5 marbles     D. 3 marbles

10. Four people divided $86 evenly between them. How much money did each person get?
    A. $19.75       B. $20.25        C. $21.50        D. $22.25

**Chapter 10**
**Lesson 1**

# Probability Lines

**GOAL**

Use probability words to describe the probability of events.

1. Describe the probability of each event as *impossible*, *possible*, or *certain*.

   a) I will have a math class this week.
   _____

   b) My hair will turn pink all on its own.
   _____

   c) It will rain on Monday. _____

   d) I will see a cat today. _____

**At-Home Help**

**Probability** describes how likely it is that an event will happen.

A **probability line** is a line, going from *impossible* to *certain*, that is used to show the probability of an event.

2. Place each event on the probability line below.

   impossible ←————————— possible ——————————→ certain

   A. I will be the only person in class tomorrow.
   B. I will have cereal for breakfast.
   C. The grass in the schoolyard will grow tomorrow.
   D. I will be younger tomorrow than I am today.

3. Describe an event that matches each probability word.
   impossible: _____
   possible: _____
   certain: _____

4. Describe each event using a probability word.

   a) The Moon will turn green next month. _____

   b) Someone in Canada will find a new job this week. _____

   c) The Sun will shine tomorrow. _____

# Conducting Spinner Experiments

**GOAL**

Conduct probability experiments using a spinner.

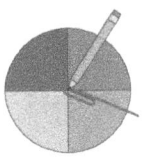

You will need a paper clip and a pencil.

**1.** Spin Spinner A 12 times. Record your results in the chart.

**Spinner A**

| Spin | 1 | 2 | 3 | 4 | 5 | 6 | 7 | 8 | 9 | 10 | 11 | 12 |
|---|---|---|---|---|---|---|---|---|---|---|---|---|
| Result | | | | | | | | | | | | |

**2.** How likely is each event if you spin Spinner A? Use the probability words *impossible*, *unlikely*, *possible*, *likely*, or *certain*.

   a) You will spin a number less than 5. _____

   b) You will spin a 6. _____

   c) You will spin an even number. _____

   d) You will spin a 1. _____

   e) You will spin a 1, 2, or 3. _____

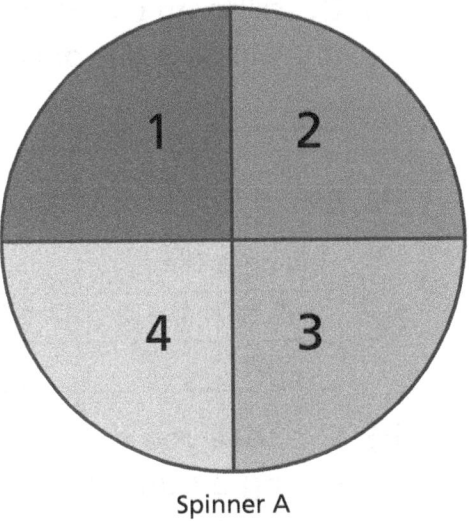

Spinner A

**3.** Place the probability of each event in Question 2 on the probability line below.

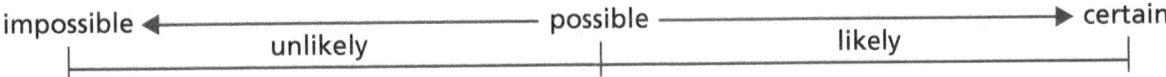

**4. a)** Suppose you spin Spinner A 10 more times. About how many times do you think you will spin an odd number?
   _____

   **b)** Test your prediction. How many times did you spin an odd number?
   _____

# Chapter 10 Lesson 3
# Conducting Experiments with a Die

**GOAL**

Conduct probability experiments using a die.

You will need a six-sided die for this activity.

**At-Home Help**

An **outcome** is the result of an experiment. For example, rolling a 3 is one possible outcome when you roll a die.

1. What outcomes are possible if you roll a die?
   _____

2. a) If you roll a die once, what is the probability that you will roll a 7? _____

   b) Describe an event that is certain to happen if you roll a die once.
   _____

3. a) Roll a die 12 times. Record your results in the chart.

   **Rolling a Die**

   | Roll | 1 | 2 | 3 | 4 | 5 | 6 | 7 | 8 | 9 | 10 | 11 | 12 |
   |---|---|---|---|---|---|---|---|---|---|---|---|---|
   | Result | | | | | | | | | | | | |

   b) Suppose you roll a die 24 times. Which is more likely: rolling a number less than 4 about 6 times OR rolling a number less than 4 about 12 times? _____

   c) Test your prediction. How many times did you roll a number less than 4? _____

4. a) Describe an experiment to test this prediction: When you roll a die, you are likely to roll a 6.
   _____
   _____

   b) Test your prediction. If you roll a die, are you likely or unlikely to roll a 6? _____

# Chapter 10 Lesson 4: Comparing Probabilities

**GOAL**

Compare probabilities and make predictions.

You will need a paper clip and a pencil.

1. Spin Spinner B 20 times. Record your results.

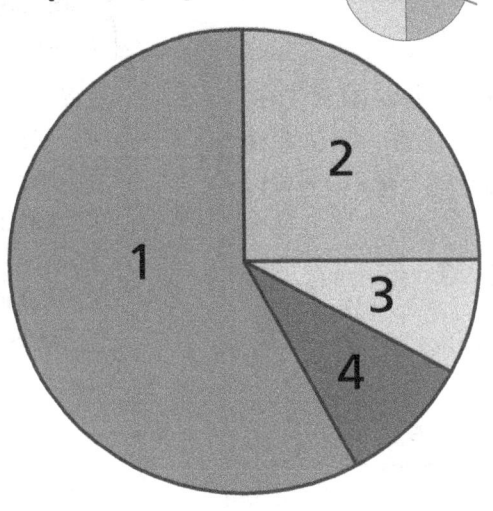

Spinner B

**At-Home Help**

Two events with the same probability of occurring are **equally likely**.

For example, if you roll a die, the probability of getting a 1 is equal to the probability of getting a 2. These events are equally likely.

**Spinner B**

| Spin | 1 | 2 | 3 | 4 | 5 | 6 | 7 | 8 | 9 | 10 | 11 | 12 | 13 | 14 | 15 | 16 | 17 | 18 | 19 | 20 |
|---|---|---|---|---|---|---|---|---|---|---|---|---|---|---|---|---|---|---|---|---|
| Result | | | | | | | | | | | | | | | | | | | | |

2. Which two numbers are equally likely to be spun with Spinner B? _____

3. Why can you predict that spinning 1 is more likely than spinning 4 with Spinner B?

_____

4. a) Use probability words to describe the probability of spinning each number with Spinner B.

1: _____    2: _____    3: _____    4: _____

b) Place the probability of spinning each number on the probability line.

impossible ←————————— possible ——————————→ certain
              unlikely                          likely

Chapter 10: Probability  **89**

# Solving Problems by Conducting Experiments

**GOAL**

Solve problems about probability.

You will need a paper bag, pennies, nickels, and dimes for this activity.

Maya put 6 coins in a paper bag. She put her hand in the bag and took out a coin, and then she put the coin back in the bag. She recorded her result on a tally chart.

Maya repeated her experiment 12 times.

Results of Taking Coins from a Bag

| penny | nickel | dime |
|---|---|---|
| ||||

**At-Home Help**

Here are some tips for conducting an experiment:
- Make sure your experiment matches what you are testing.
- Record your results.
- Repeat your experiment several times.

1. Which of these two bags do you think Maya used for her experiment? Explain your thinking.

   _____
   _____
   _____

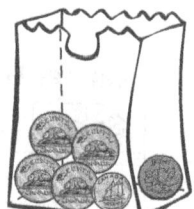

Bag 1: 4 pennies, 1 nickel, 1 dime

Bag 2: 4 nickels, 1 penny, 1 dime

2. **a)** Conduct Maya's experiment. Record your results in the tally charts.

**Results of Taking Coins from Bag 1**

| Penny | Nickel | Dime |
|---|---|---|
|  |  |  |

**Results of Taking Coins from Bag 2**

| Penny | Nickel | Dime |
|---|---|---|
|  |  |  |

**b)** Use your results to decide which bag Maya most likely used for her experiment.

_____
_____

# Chapter 10 Lesson 6: Designing Spinners

**GOAL**

Design spinners to match probabilities.

You will need a paper clip and a pencil.

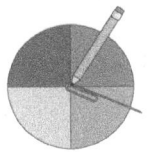

1. **a)** Design a spinner to match each probability rule. Use the circles on this page.

    **A.** Two sections: Section 1 is very likely. Section 2 is very unlikely.

    **B.** Three sections: Section 1 is unlikely. Sections 2 and 3 are equally likely.

   **b)** Test the spinner you made for rule A. Does it match the probability rule? Explain.

   _____
   _____

   **c)** Test the spinner you made for rule B. Does it match the probability rule? Explain.

   _____
   _____

**At-Home Help**

You can design a spinner to match a probability rule.

For example:
"There are three sections. Section 1 is very likely. Sections 2 and 3 are very unlikely."

- My spinner needs to have three sections.
- I will draw section 1 to be very large, so it is very likely. I will draw sections 2 and 3 to be very small, so they are unlikely.
- I will test my spinner.

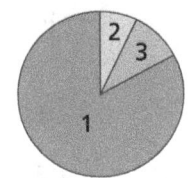

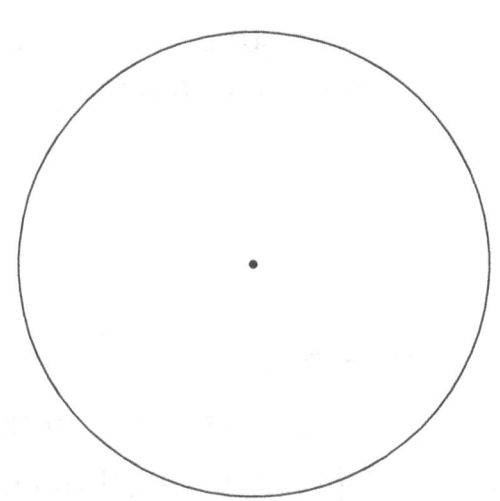
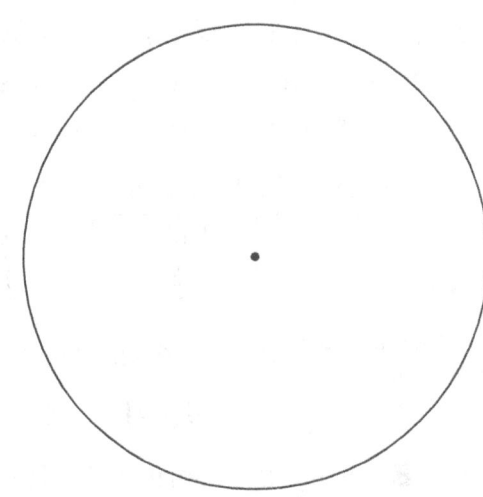

# Chapter 10   Test Yourself

**Circle the correct answer.**

1. What is the probability that your eyebrows will disappear in the night?

   A. impossible   B. unlikely   C. likely   D. certain

2. What is the probability that at least one person in Canada will go to school this year?

   A. impossible   B. unlikely   C. likely   D. certain

3. Jolie spun Spinner D six times and got these results:

   Spinning Spinner D

   | Spin | 1 | 2 | 3 | 4 | 5 | 6 |
   |---|---|---|---|---|---|---|
   | Result | 2 | 2 | 2 | 1 | 2 | 2 |

   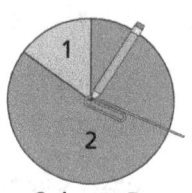
   Spinner D

   Next, Jolie spun Spinner D once. How likely is it that she got a 2?

   A. impossible   B. unlikely   C. likely   D. certain

4. Tai rolled a die 12 times and got these results.

   Rolling a Die

   | Roll | 1 | 2 | 3 | 4 | 5 | 6 | 7 | 8 | 9 | 10 | 11 | 12 |
   |---|---|---|---|---|---|---|---|---|---|---|---|---|
   | Result | 1 | 4 | 2 | 6 | 5 | 3 | 2 | 6 | 1 | 5 | 4 | 3 |

   Next, Tai rolled a die once. How likely is it that he rolled a 6?

   A. impossible   B. unlikely   C. likely   D. certain

5. Ami put three coins in a paper bag. She pulled out a coin, and then put it back in the bag. She repeated this experiment nine times. Ami's results are in the chart.

   Results of Taking Coins Out of the Bag

   | Penny | Nickel | Dime |
   |---|---|---|
   | 0 | 3 | 6 |

   Which bag did Ami most likely use for her experiment?

   A. Bag 1: 1 nickel, 2 dimes       C. Bag 3: 2 pennies, 1 nickel
   B. Bag 2: 1 penny, 1 nickel, 1 dime   D. Bag 4: 2 nickels, 1 dime

# Chapter 11 Lesson 1: Vertical and Horizontal Lines and Faces

## GOAL

Identify and draw horizontal and vertical lines, edges, and faces.

You will need a red pencil crayon and a blue pencil crayon.

**At-Home Help**

**Horizontal** describes a line, a face (a flat surface), or the edge of an object that goes straight across.

**Vertical** describes a line, a face, or the edge of an object that goes straight up and down.

1. Label each edge or face as horizontal or vertical.

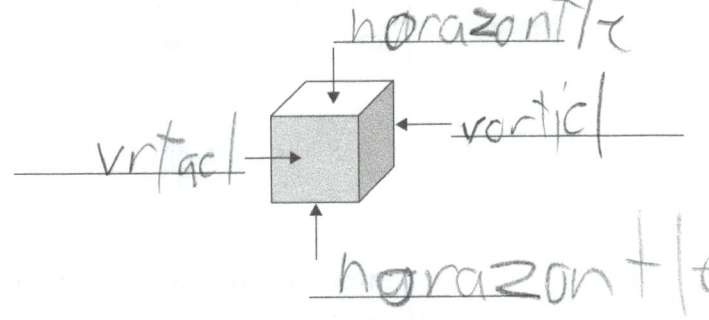

horazontlc
vrtacl
varticl
horazontle

2. Circle each horizontal line in the drawing to the right with a blue pencil. Draw an X on each vertical line with a red pencil.

3. Colour one horizontal face on the object below blue. Colour one vertical face red.

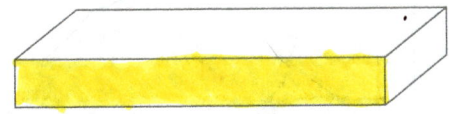

4. Find an object at home with horizontal and vertical faces. Sketch the object.

   a) Colour one horizontal face blue.
   b) Circle each horizontal edge.
   c) Colour one vertical face red.
   d) Draw an X on each vertical edge.

# Chapter 11 Lesson 2: Parallel, Intersecting, and Perpendicular Lines and Faces

**GOAL**

Identify and draw parallel, intersecting, and perpendicular lines, edges, and faces.

You will need a small box.

1. a) Mark the parallel lines in this diagram with arrows.

   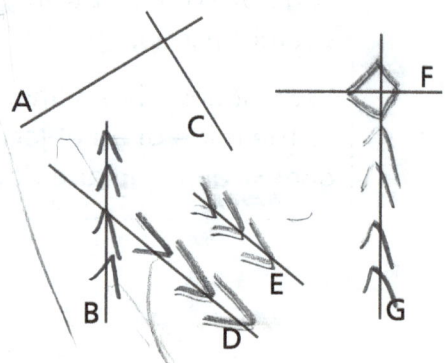

   b) Mark the perpendicular lines with a square corner.

   c) Which lines are parallel to each other?
   ED

   d) Which lines are perpendicular to each other?
   FG

2. Find a small box that looks like the rectangular prism in the diagram. Use the box to help you label the parts of the diagram.

   a) Draw Xs on a pair of parallel vertical edges.

   b) Draw circles on a pair of parallel horizontal edges.

   c) Draw triangles on a pair of perpendicular edges.

   d) Use your pencil to shade one vertical face.

   e) Draw stars on a pair of perpendicular faces.

**At-Home Help**

Parallel lines or faces do not meet. They are always the same distance apart. Parallel lines are marked with arrows.

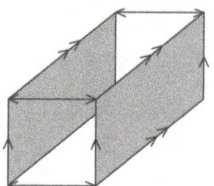

Intersecting lines or faces meet or cross.

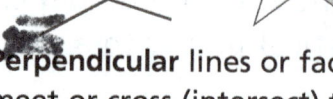

Perpendicular lines or faces meet or cross (intersect) to make a square corner.

square corner

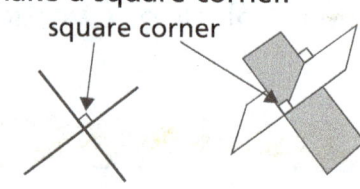

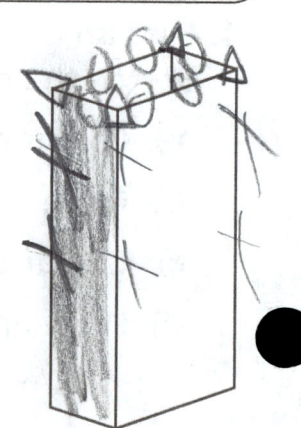

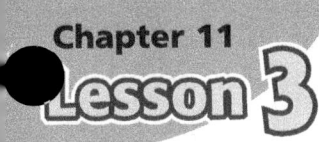

# Finding Lines and Faces in the Media

**GOAL**

Identify relationships between lines in 2-D faces and faces in 3-D objects.

You will need a ruler and red, blue, and yellow pencil crayons.

1. Identify vertical and horizontal faces in the drawing.

    a) Colour three vertical faces red.

    b) Colour three horizontal faces blue.

2. Identify parallel, intersecting, and perpendicular lines in the drawing. Use your ruler to help you.

    a) Circle two pairs of parallel lines.

    b) Draw Xs on two pairs of perpendicular lines.

3. Identify parallel and perpendicular faces in the drawing.

    a) Colour one pair of parallel faces yellow.

    b) Draw stars on one pair of perpendicular faces.

# Chapter 11 Lesson 4: Sorting Quadrilaterals

**GOAL**

Sort quadrilaterals according to their attributes.

1. Which of these shapes are quadrilaterals?

   _____

   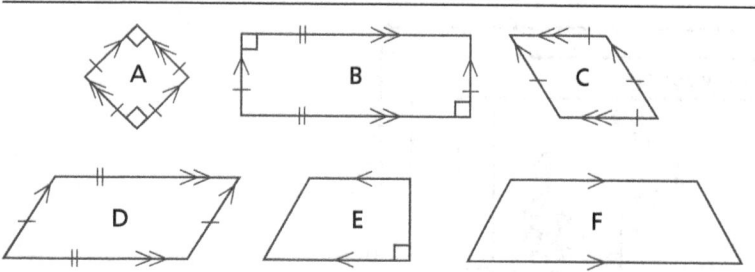

2. Identify two examples of each quadrilateral from the shapes in Question 1:

   trapezoid _____

   parallelogram _____

   rhombus _____

3. Sort the quadrilaterals in Question 1 by sketching them in the Venn diagram below.

   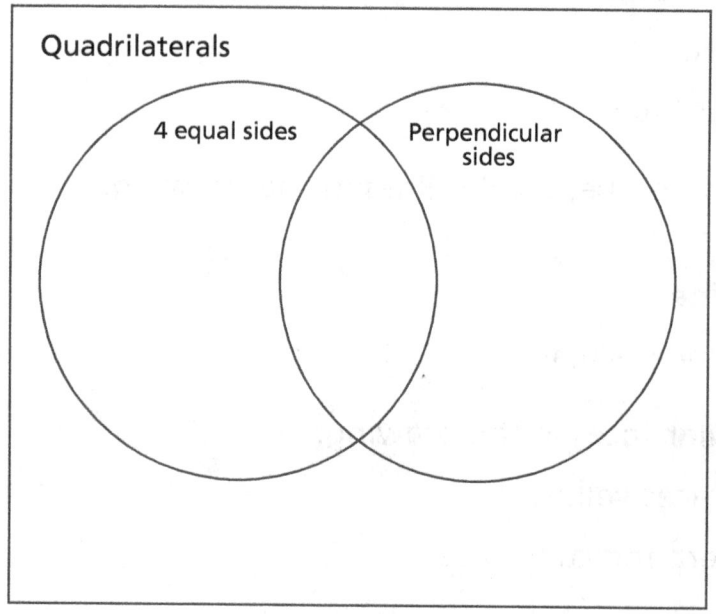

### At-Home Help

A **quadrilateral** is a polygon (a closed 2-D shape) with four straight sides.

A **trapezoid** is a quadrilateral with only one pair of parallel sides. (The arrows show parallel sides.)

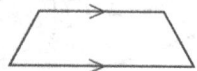

A **parallelogram** is a quadrilateral with opposite sides that are parallel and equal. (The hatchmarks show equal sides.)

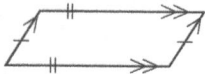

A **rhombus** is a parallelogram with four equal sides.

# Solving Problems by Drawing Diagrams

**GOAL**

Draw diagrams to solve problems.

1. Draw a diagram to solve each riddle.

   a) I am a quadrilateral.
      I have only one pair of parallel sides.
      I have no square corners.

   b) I am a quadrilateral.
      I have four equal sides.
      I have parallel sides.
      I have no perpendicular sides.

   c) I am a quadrilateral.
      I have two pairs of equal sides.
      I have no perpendicular sides.

   d) I am a quadrilateral.
      I have one pair of parallel sides.
      I have two square corners.

2. a) Draw a quadrilateral. Then create a riddle for your quadrilateral by describing its sides and the number of square corners it has.

   b) Ask a friend or family member to guess your riddle.

# Chapter 11   Test Yourself

**Circle the correct answer.**

1. Which lines in the diagram are horizontal?

    A. lines A and B
    C. lines C and D
    B. lines B and C
    D. lines A and E

    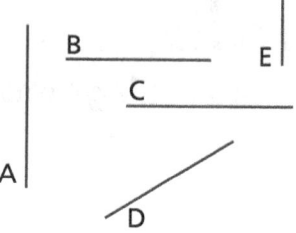

2. Which face or faces in the rectangular prism are vertical?

    A. the white face
    B. the light grey faces
    C. the dark grey faces
    D. the light grey and the dark grey faces

3. Which streets are perpendicular?

    A. Ama and Bark Streets
    B. Cor and Ama Streets
    C. Ama and Derry Streets
    D. Bark and Cor Streets

4. Which shape is a trapezoid?

    A.
    C.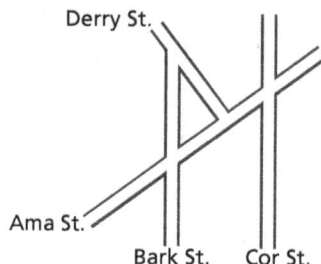
    B.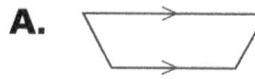
    D.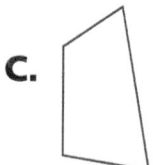

5. Jolie drew a quadrilateral. It had two pairs of equal sides, and no perpendicular sides. Which shape did she draw?

    A. a square    B. a rhombus    C. a rectangle    D. a parallelogram

98    Nelson Math Focus 5 Workbook